Microsoft Windows 2000 Active Directory Lab Manual

Joseph P. Sellers
and David Neilan

COURSE
TECHNOLOGY
™
THOMSON LEARNING

Australia • Canada • Mexico • Singapore • Spain • United Kingdom • United States

COURSE
TECHNOLOGY
TM
THOMSON LEARNING

Microsoft Windows 2000 Active Directory Lab Manual
by Joseph P. Sellers and David Neilan

Product Manager:
Laura Hildebrand

Quality Assurance Manager:
John Bosco

Text Designer:
GEX Publishing Services

Technical Editor:
Jim Taylor

Associate Product Manager:
Tim Gleeson

Compositor:
GEX Publishing Services

Production Editor:
Brooke Albright

Editorial Assistant:
Nick Lombardi

Cover Design:
Efrat Reis

Developmental Editor:
Moirag Haddad

Marketing Manager:
Toby Shelton

TABLE OF CONTENTS

CHAPTER TEN
IMPLEMENTING GROUP POLICY 135

CHAPTER ELEVEN
MANAGING USER ENVIRONMENTS WITH GROUP POLICY 151

CHAPTER TWELVE
DEPLOYING AND MANAGING SOFTWARE USING GROUP POLICY 179

INTRODUCTION

The objective of this lab manual is to assist you in preparing for the Microsoft certification exam # 70-217: *Implementing and Administering a Microsoft Windows 2000 Directory Services Infrastructure* by applying the Windows 2000 Active Directory objectives to relevant lab activities. This text is designed to be used in conjunction with *MCSE Guide to Microsoft Windows 2000 Active Directory* (0-619-01600-0), but it also can be used to supplement any MCSE courseware. Although this manual is written to be used in a classroom lab environment, it also may be used for self-study on a home network.

FEATURES

In order to ensure a successful experience for instructors and students alike, this book includes the following features:

- **Lab Objectives** – Every lab has a brief description and list of learning objectives.
- **Materials Required** – Every lab includes information on hardware, software, and other materials you will need to complete the lab.
- **Activity Sections** – Labs are presented in manageable sections. Where appropriate, additional Activity Background information is provided to illustrate the importance of a particular project.
- **Step-by-Step Instructions** – Steps provide practice, which enhances technical proficiency.
- **Microsoft Windows 2000 Directory Services Infrastructure MCSE Certification objectives** – For each chapter, the relevant objectives from MCSE Exam # 70-217 are listed.

HARDWARE REQUIREMENTS

- A Pentium 166 MHz CPU or higher
- 256 MB of RAM recommended (128 MB minimum)
- A 2GB hard disk with at least 1 GB of available storage space
- A CD-ROM drive
- A modem (optional)
- A printer (optional)

SOFTWARE/SETUP REQUIREMENTS

- Access to a Windows 2000 Server or Windows 2000 Advanced Server system with updated Internet Explorer 5.5 and Active Directory installed.
- Internet Access
- Access to *Windows 2000 Server Resource Kit, Supplement 1*

CHAPTER ONE

INTRODUCTION TO ACTIVE DIRECTORY

Labs included in this chapter

➤ Lab 1.1 Working with Microsoft Management Console (MMC)

➤ Lab 1.2 Viewing the Local Group Policy

➤ Lab 1.3 Active Directory Users and Computers

Microsoft MCSE Exam #70-217 Objectives	
Objective	Lab
Installing and Configuring Active Directory	1.3
Installing, Configuring, Managing, Monitoring, and Troubleshooting DNS for Active Directory	1.1
Configuring, Managing, Monitoring, Optimizing, and Troubleshooting Change and Configuration Management	1.2, 1.3
Managing, Monitoring, and Optimizing the Components of Active Directory	1.1
Configuring, Managing, Monitoring, and Troubleshooting Security in a Directory Services Infrastructure	1.1, 1.3

LAB SCENARIO

The Labs in this chapter will introduce the student to some of the available Active Directory management interfaces.

LAB 1.1 WORKING WITH MICROSOFT MANAGEMENT CONSOLE (MMC)

Objectives

The goal of this lab is to show how to create an MMC to allow the student to access administrative items on the local machine. After completing this lab, you will be able to:

➤ Create and manage an MMC (Microsoft Management Console).

Materials Required

This lab will require the following:

➤ Access to *MCSE Guide to Microsoft Windows 2000 Active Directory*

Activity Prerequisites

Have access to a Windows 2000 Server machine.

ACTIVITY

Use the following steps to create and save a custom MMC.

1. Log on to the computer using the username and password assigned to you.

2. Click **Start**, click **Run**, and then type **mmc** in the dialog box and press **Enter**.

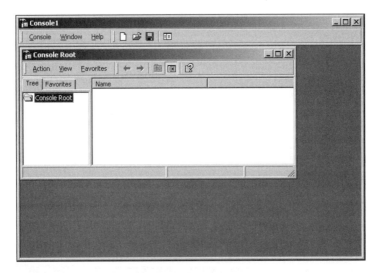

Figure 1-1   An empty MMC console

3. In the Console1 dialog box, click **Console**, and then click **Add/Remove Snap-in**.

4. In the Add/Remove Snap-in dialog box, click **Add**.

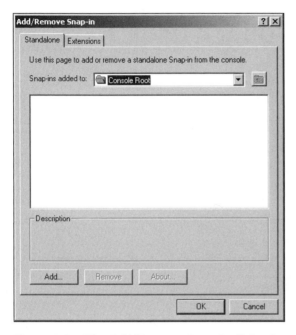

Figure 1-2   The Add/Remove Snap-in dialog box

5. Scroll down the Available Standalone Snap-ins list, choose **Group Policy**, and then click **Add**.

6. Click **Finish**, click **Close**, and then click **OK**.

7. You now have an MMC configured to show the Local Computer Policy.

8. Click **Console**, click **Save As**, and then click **Desktop** from the drop-down list. Name the new console **Local Policy** and click **Save**.

9. Close the remaining dialog box.

LAB 1.2 VIEWING THE LOCAL GROUP POLICY

Objectives

The goal of this lab is to use an MMC to access some of the administrative interfaces available. After completing this lab, you will be able to:

➤ Access the Local Group Policy settings through a previously defined MMC.

Materials Required

This lab will require the following:

➤ Access to *MCSE Guide to Microsoft Windows 2000 Active Directory*

Activity Prerequisites

Have access to a Windows 2000 Server machine that was used in the previous Lab.

ACTIVITY

Follow the next set of steps to access your system's Local Security Policy.

1. Make sure you are logged on to the same computer with the username and password used in the previous Lab.

2. Double-click the **Local Policy.msc** icon on the desktop.

3. Expand the **Console Root** dialog box.

4. Expand the **Local Computer Policy**, and then expand **Computer Configuration**.

5. Expand **Windows Settings**, and then expand **Security Settings**.

6. Expand **Account Policies**, and then expand **Password Policy**.

The dialog box shows some of the settings that are used by the operating system to control the behavior of the security components used during logon access.

These settings are local in this case, but the same type of settings and style of MMC are used when accessing an Active Directory-enabled machine.

View these items, but do not make any changes, as this could cause undesirable effects later on.

7. Close all open dialog boxes without saving any settings.

8. Log off.

LAB 1.3 ACTIVE DIRECTORY USERS AND COMPUTERS

Objectives

The goal of this lab is to familiarize the student with an MMC configured to show the Active Directory Users and Computers interface. After completing this lab, you will be able to:

➤ Access information and settings in the Active Directory.

➤ Use Windows 2000 tools for administration.

Materials Required

This lab will require the following:

➤ Access to *MCSE Guide to Microsoft Windows 2000 Active Directory*

Activity Prerequisites

Have access to a machine that is part of an Active Directory domain, either as a member server or a domain controller.

ACTIVITY

Open a custom MMC that gives access to Active Directory Users and Computers and provides information about a User Account object.

1. Log on to the computer using the username and password assigned to you.

2. Click **Start**, click **Run**, and then type **mmc**. Press **Enter**.

3. In the Console1 dialog box, click **Console**, and then click **Add/Remove Snap-in**.

4. In the Add/Remove Snap-in dialog box, click **Add**.

5. Scroll down the Available Standalone Snap-ins list, choose **Active Directory Users and Computers**, and then click **Add**. See Figure 1-3.

6. Click **Close**, and then click **OK**.

7. You now have an MMC configured to show the Active Directory Users and Computers interface.

Figure 1-3   Viewing the various snap-in modules available on the computer

If the machine you are working on is a domain controller, this MMC would be available to you through the Administrative Tools menu as a previously configured snap-in.

8. Expand the **Console Root** dialog box.

9. Expand the **Active Directory Users and Computers** subtree, and open the domain below.

10. Double-click the **Users** folder. You can see a listing of default user accounts and groups within the domain. Probably you can also see other user accounts and groups that have been added to the domain by the Administrator.

11. Double-click one of the user accounts and look at some of the properties associated with the account.

12. Click on the available tabs and look at some examples of the information associated with a User type object.

13. Record which tab would show Group Membership.

14. Record which tab would display information about a possible logon script.

View these items, but do not make any changes, as this could cause undesirable effects later on.

15. Click **OK** to close the active dialog box and return to Active Directory Users and Computers.

16. Click the **Domain Controllers** node to view the DCs of your domain.

17. Record the other nodes or folders available for viewing.

18. Close all open dialog boxes.

19. Log off.

CHAPTER TWO

VIEWING ACTIVE DIRECTORY COMPONENTS

Labs included in this chapter

➤ Lab 2.1 Active Directory Sites and Services

➤ Lab 2.2 Active Directory Domains and Trusts

Microsoft MCSE Exam #70-217 Objectives	
Objective	**Lab**
Installing and Configuring Active Directory	2.1, 2.2
Configuring, Managing, Monitoring, Optimizing, and Troubleshooting Change and Configuration Management	2.1, 2.2
Managing, Monitoring, and Optimizing the Components of Active Directory	2.1, 2.2
Configuring, Managing, Monitoring, and Troubleshooting Security in a Directory Services Infrastructure	2.2

LAB SCENARIO

The Labs in this chapter will give the student an introduction to more of the available Active Directory management interfaces.

LAB 2.1 ACTIVE DIRECTORY SITES AND SERVICES

Objectives

The goal of this lab is to show the available interfaces and the information displayed through the supplied management consoles. After completing this lab, you will be able to:

> ➤ Open and view AD information through the Sites and Services MMC.

Materials Required

This lab will require the following:

> ➤ Access to *MCSE Guide to Microsoft Windows 2000 Active Directory*

Activity Prerequisites

Have access to a Windows 2000 server that is either a member of a domain or a domain controller.

ACTIVITY

Use the following steps to activate a Sites and Services MMC.

1. Log on to the computer with the username and password assigned to you. If you are logging on to a domain controller, proceed to Step **8**.

2. Click **Start**, click **Run**, and then type **mmc** in the dialog box and press **Enter**.

3. In the Console1 dialog box, click **Console** and then click **Add/Remove Snap-in**.

4. In the Add/Remove Snap-in dialog box, click **Add**.

5. Scroll through the Available Standalone Snap-ins list, choose **Active Directory Sites and Services**, and then click **Add**. See Figure 2-1.

6. Click **Close**, and then click **OK**.

7. Proceed to Step 9.

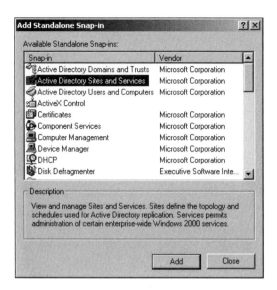

Figure 2-1   Viewing the various snap-in modules available in the Add Standalone Snap-in dialog box

You do not need to follow Step 8 unless you were logging on to a domain controller in Step 1, at which point you proceeded to Step 8.

8. Click **Start**, point to **Programs**, point to **Administrative Tools**, and then click **Active Directory Sites and Services**.

9. You now have an MMC configured to show the Sites and Services interface. In the console window, expand the **Active Directory Sites and Services** node, as shown in Figure 2-2.

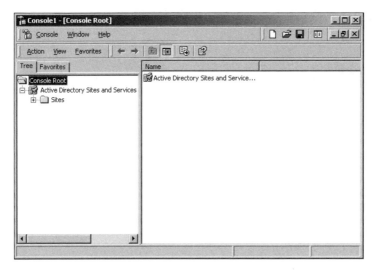

Figure 2-2   The Active Directory Sites and Services node expanded

10. Expand the **Sites** tree. (See Figure 2-3.) You should be able to see at least the three following sub-objects:

■ Default–First–Site–Name

■ Inter–Site Transports

■ Subnets

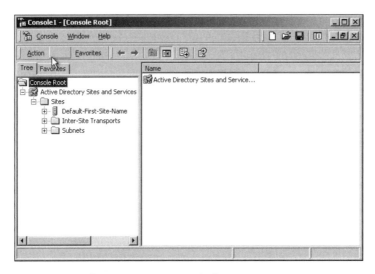

Figure 2-3   The Sites tree expanded

11. Expand the **Default–First–Site–Name** node as shown in Figure 2-4. What is now displayed?

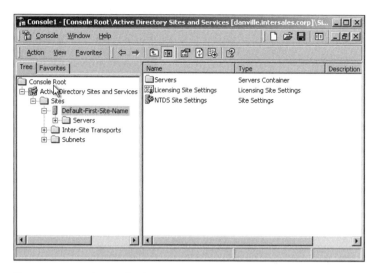

Figure 2-4   The Default-First-Site-Name node expanded

12. Expand the sub-folder. How many machines are listed?

13. What type of machine is listed?

14. Expand one of the Servers. What do you see now?

15. Minimize the Default-First-Site-Name node.

16. Expand the **Inter-Site Transports** node as shown in Figure 2-5. What do you see?

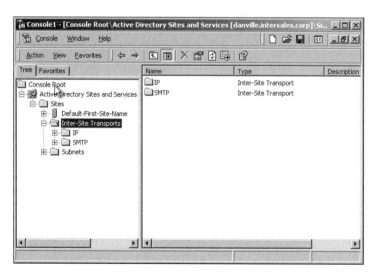

Figure 2-5   The Inter-Site Transports node expanded

17. Expand the **IP** node. Within this you should see the **DEFAULTIPSITELINK** connector, as shown in Figure 2-6. This is the first connector created to link domain controllers when an Active Directory domain is connected. There could be more than one.

18. Expand the **SMTP** node. Within this you might see special connectors that link sites using SMTP as the transport protocol. Whether you see any connectors depends on how the network and domain structure has been implemented.

19. The final node is the **Subnets** folder, which contains information related to other sites' TCP/IP subnet addressing and the sites supported by it.

20. Close all dialog boxes and log off.

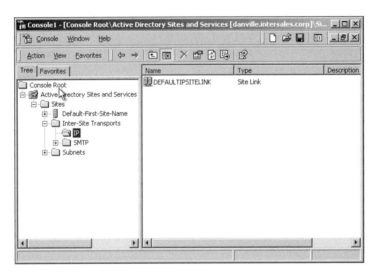

Figure 2-6   The DEFAULTIPSITELINK connector within the IP node

LAB 2.2 ACTIVE DIRECTORY DOMAINS AND TRUSTS

Objectives

The goal of this lab is to become familiar with the Active Directory administrative tools. After completing this lab, you will be able to:

➤ Use the Active Directory Domains and Trusts MMC.

Materials Required

This lab will require the following:

➤ Access to *MCSE Guide to Microsoft Windows 2000 Active Directory*

Activity Prerequisites

Have access to a Windows 2000 server that is either a member of a domain or a domain controller.

2

ACTIVITY

Use the following steps to activate an Active Directory Domains and Trusts MMC.

1. Log on to the computer with the username and password assigned to you. If you are logging on to a domain controller, proceed to Step **8**.

2. Click **Start**, click **Run**, and then type **mmc** in the dialog box and press **Enter**.

3. In the Console1 dialog box, click **Console** and then click **Add/Remove Snap-in**.

4. In the Add/Remove Snap-in dialog box, click **Add**.

5. Scroll through the Available Standalone Snap-ins list, choose **Active Directory Domains and Trusts**, and then click **Add**. See Figure 2-7.

Figure 2-7   The list of Available Standalone Snap-ins

6. Click **Close**, and then click **OK**.

7. Proceed to Step 9.

You do not need to follow Step 8 unless you were logging on to a domain controller in Step 1, at which point you proceeded to Step 8.

8. Click **Start**, point to **Programs**, point to **Administrative Tools**, and click **Active Directory Domains and Trusts**.

9. You now have an MMC configured to show the Domains and Trusts interface.

10. In the console window, expand the **Active Directory Domains and Trusts** node. See Figure 2-8. You should now see your domain.

11. Right-click your domain and choose **Manage**. What happens?

12. Close the active dialog box and return to the Domains and Trusts console.

13. Right-click your domain and click **Properties**. This now displays the many properties associated with your domain. See Figure 2-9.

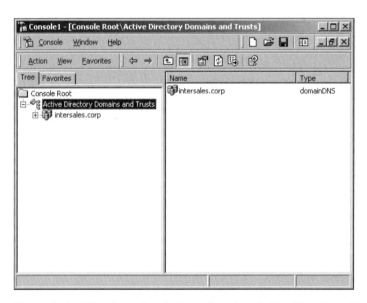

Figure 2-8   The Console window showing Active Directory Domains and Trusts expanded

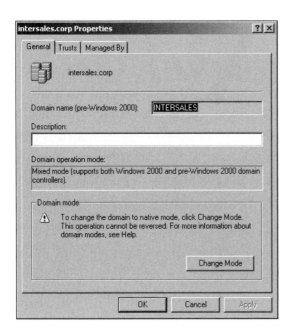

Figure 2-9   Viewing the mode that the domain is running in

14. What mode is your domain running in?

15. What (if any) trust relationships are there?

16. Close all open dialog boxes without saving any settings.

17. Log off.

CHAPTER THREE

PLANNING AN ACTIVE DIRECTORY IMPLEMENTATION

Labs included in this chapter
➤ Lab 3.1 Working with Single Domains
➤ Lab 3.2 Organizing Trees
➤ Lab 3.3 Using Forests
➤ Lab 3.4 Adapting to Expansion
➤ Lab 3.5 Gathering Information

Microsoft MCSE Exam #70-217 Objectives	
Objective	**Lab**
Installing and Configuring Active Directory	3.1, 3.2, 3.3, 3.4
Installing, Configuring, Managing, Monitoring, and Troubleshooting DNS for Active Directory	3.1, 3.2, 3.3, 3.4
Configuring, Managing, Monitoring, Optimizing, and Troubleshooting Change and Configuration Management	3.1, 3.2, 3.4, 3.5
Managing, Monitoring, and Optimizing the Components of Active Directory	3.1, 3.2, 3.3, 3.4, 3.5
Configuring, Managing, Monitoring, and Troubleshooting Security in a Directory Services Infrastructure	3.1, 3.2, 3.3, 3.4, 3.5

LAB SCENARIO

The labs in this chapter will present designs and implementation proposals. A scenario will be introduced to assist the student in understanding the functions and differences among the following Active Directory design components:

➤ Domains

➤ Sites

➤ Trees

➤ Forests

➤ DNS namespaces

The labs for chapter 3 focus on three companies:

➤ FixitUp Ltd., a medium-sized builders' supply company

➤ WordwideTravel Ltd., a travel agency that specializes in tours and travel to remote locations

➤ DangerousTours Ltd., a travel agency with a specific clientele who enjoy dangerous sports

These companies are typical of many businesses deploying Windows 2000 and organizing their networks using domains, trees, and forests.

LAB 3.1 WORKING WITH SINGLE DOMAINS

Objectives

The goal of this lab is to show how a single domain is utilized. After completing this lab, you will be able to:

➤ Identify the reasons for placement and design of a single domain and site configuration.

➤ Identify how a domain enables a single contained company to control its network.

➤ Examine the relationship between domains and DNS namespaces.

Materials Required

This lab will require the following:

➤ Access to *MCSE Guide to Microsoft Windows 2000 Active Directory*

Activity Prerequisites

There are no prerequisites for this activity.

ACTIVITY

Read the following scenario and answer the questions that follow. This scenario is very common for small self-contained companies and is the easiest to set up and administer.

This design/planning session will focus on the basic building block, the domain. FixitUp Ltd. is a medium-sized builders' supply company, with one location and no partners, subsidiaries, or external influences. They have 25 client systems connecting to four main servers. The four domain servers provide all of the application, file, and print services.

3

1. What sort of domain structure should be used?

2. Would there be any advantage to implementing multiple sites in this scenario?

3. Give an example of a possible Internal DNS namespace.

4. How many domain controllers would you recommend?

LAB 3.2 ORGANIZING TREES

Objectives

The goal of this lab is to show how two or more domains create a tree. After completing this lab, you will be able to:

➤ Explain the differences between multiple domains, and multiple domains within a single tree structure.

➤ Understand the relationship between domains that are linked in a hierarchical tree structure, and when to use such a design.

Materials Required

This lab will require the following:

➤ Access to *MCSE Guide to Microsoft Windows 2000 Active Directory*

Activity Prerequisites

There are no prerequisites for this activity.

Active Directory sites, replication, and the type of connections used for WANs will be covered in later labs.

ACTIVITY

Read the following scenario and answer the questions that follow.

WordwideTravel Ltd. is a travel agency that specializes in tours and travel to remote locations. The head office is located in Vancouver, with 3 smaller offices in Iqaluit (Nunavut), Alexandria (Egypt), and Sydney (Australia). There are approximately 50 people in each office and the company is wholly owned by the Vancouver partners. The company has grown by amalgamation, and the locations are all still controlled and administered locally.

1. What sort of Domain structure could be implemented?

2. If each of the locations has only one subnet and fast LAN access, how many sites in total would they ideally need?

3. Based on the Head office DNS namespace of WorldWideTravel.com, how would the DNS namespace be shown at the other locations?

LAB 3.3 USING FORESTS

Objectives

The goal of this lab is to show that two or more domain trees can be joined to form a forest. After completing this lab, you will be able to:

➤ Understand how forests are used in domains.

➤ Understand how multiple trees are used to create a forest, allowing companies with dissimilar DNS namespaces to co-operate and co-exist.

Materials Required

This lab will require the following:

➤ Access to *MCSE Guide to Microsoft Windows 2000 Active Directory*

Activity Prerequisites

There are no prerequisites for this activity.

ACTIVITY

Read the following scenario and answer the questions that follow.

A new Travel organization, DangerousTours Ltd., has entered into partnership with WorldwideTours Ltd. DangerousTours has its head office in San Diego (Hiking in Death Valley), with offices in Arizona (Freefall parachuting in the Grand Canyon) and Louisiana

(Gator wrestling). The companies wish to remain separate, but work closely, accessing and selling each other's tours.

1. How would these factors affect the two companies' present Active Directory designs?

2. How could the two domain configurations be joined?

3. What would the overall DNS namespace look like if DangerousTours Ltd. uses DangerousTours.com as its namespace?

LAB 3.4 ADAPTING TO EXPANSION

Objectives

The goal of this lab is to help you understand the building blocks that go into making a domain and what can happen when a company or organization expands. After completing this lab, you will be able to:

➤ Address the expansion requirements of a growing domain.

Materials Required

This lab will require the following:

➤ Access to *MCSE Guide to Microsoft Windows 2000 Active Directory*

➤ Internet connectivity to allow connection to the Microsoft web site

Activity Prerequisites

There are no prerequisites for this activity.

ACTIVITY

Read the following information and answer the questions that follow.

FixitUp Ltd., the builders' supply company you first encountered in Lab 3.1, has purchased the rights to a new tool that is revolutionizing the Do-It-Yourself market. Nearly overnight the company has reached multi-million-dollar sales, and has begun rapid expansion. As part of this expansion, they have opened 60 new stores, each having an office with about 20 staff.

They have fast network connections between all of these offices and now need to modify their domain design to take all of these changes into account.

1. As they have very little experience with AD domains yet, how can they organize their present domain to ease the administrative overhead without moving into multi-site or multi-domain designs?

2. How would these changes affect the current DNS namespace ?

3. Would there be any need to set up AD site connectors or trust relationships?

4. Domain controllers provide authentication services. Keeping in mind the small number of users at each location and the relatively high-speed connections between locations, what are the most obvious ways of providing these authentication services to the users?

5. Use your web browser to connect to the following URL:
   http://www.microsoft.com/technet/treeview/default.asp?url=/TechNet/ prodtechnol/windows2000serv/proddocs/adguide/adplan.asp

   What is the general topic of this web content ?

6. Here is another URL that provides information about planning:
   http://www.microsoft.com/technet/treeview/default.asp?url=/TechNet/ prodtechnol/windows2000serv/proddocs/adguide/adbranch.asp?frame=true

   Using the information and examples provided in the above web links, list a few of the other expansion possibilities.

LAB 3.5 GATHERING INFORMATION

Objectives

The goal of this lab is to help you understand what information is required before you can effectively design an Active Directory domain. After completing this lab, you will be able to:

➤ Gather information that will help you create an Active Directory design.

Materials Required

This lab will require the following:

➤ Access to *MCSE Guide to Microsoft Windows 2000 Active Directory*

➤ Internet connectivity to allow connection to the Microsoft web site

Activity Prerequisites

There are no prerequisites for this activity.

ACTIVITY

Using your company, or another company you have knowledge of, as an example, gather information that will help you design an Active Directory domain. Use the example shown following and expand it as required.

Table 3-1   Information for planning an Active Directory domain

Country	City	Office	Network Link	Task	Number of Users
CA	Winnipeg	Pembina	128Kb Frame 3Mb Wireless	Manufacturing	200
CA	Winnipeg	Bannatyne	10Mb Fiber Internet Virtual Private Network 3Mb Wireless	Accounting Administration Sales	20
USA	Minneapolis	Main Street	10Mb Fiber 256Kb Frame	Design Sales	90
Mexico	Chihuahua	Aldama	56Kb Frame	Manufacturing	50
UK	Swindon	Park South	Internet Virtual Private Network	Sales	20

Another good planning aid would be a diagram showing the current or proposed network layout. A sample diagram is shown in Figure 3-1.

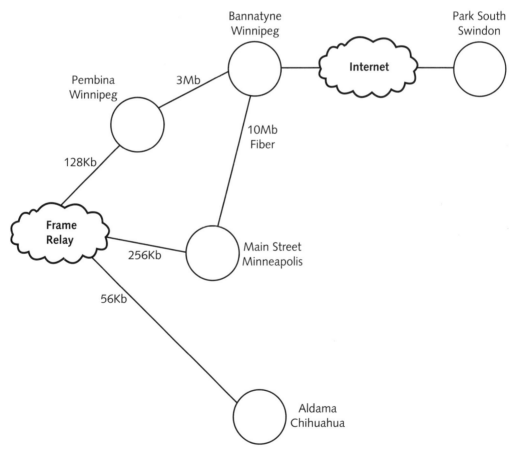

Figure 3-1   Diagram representing network information

Although these are basic examples, they do show some of the information required to create an Active Directory domain plan. Other things that would dictate or direct the design include the organization of the current company, the location of administrative staff, network reliability, network costs, differences in security requirements, and company plans for growth.

A resource for this type of planning can be found on the Microsoft web site at:

http://www.microsoft.com/technet/downloads/exe/adboja01.exe

There you will find a complete outline of the type of information that is necessary and the decisions required to create a domain plan.

INSTALLING AND
TROUBLESHOOTING DNS

Labs included in this chapter

➤ Lab 4.1 Gathering Information

➤ Lab 4.2 Installing DNS

➤ Lab 4.3 Configuring DNS

➤ Lab 4.4 Adding Records

➤ Lab 4.5 Monitoring a DNS Implementation

➤ Lab 4.6 Troubleshooting a DNS Implementation

Microsoft MCSE Exam #70-217 Objectives	
Objective	**Lab**
Installing, Configuring, Managing, Monitoring, and Troubleshooting DNS for Active Directory	4.1, 4.2, 4.3, 4.4, 4.5
Managing, Monitoring, and Optimizing the Components of Active Directory	4.3, 4.6
Configuring, Managing, Monitoring, and Troubleshooting Security in a Directory Services Infrastructure	4.3, 4.4, 4.5, 4.6

LAB SCENARIO

The Labs in this chapter are based upon Active Directory's requirement for Domain Name Service (DNS), covering pre-installation planning through post-installation troubleshooting.

LAB 4.1 GATHERING INFORMATION

Objectives

The goal of this lab is to gather information required to plan the design and installation of a DNS implementation that will support a Microsoft Windows 2000 Active Directory domain. After completing this lab, you will be able to:

> ➤ Use this information to plan the design and installation of a DNS implementation.

Materials Required

This lab will require the following:

> ➤ Access to *MCSE Guide to Microsoft Windows 2000 Active Directory*

> ➤ Paper, pen, pencils, or a whiteboard

Activity Prerequisites

There are no prerequisites for this activity.

ACTIVITY

Gather or create the following information for use in these labs:

1. Internal domain name (e.g., *YourDNSname*.com). The name does not have to match the external DNS name and can be almost anything. For these labs, use your own internal DNS name whenever you see *YourDNSname*.com.

2. Internal IP address subnets and mask (e.g., 192.168.0.0 with a mask of 255.255.0.0)

3. IP address information of internal systems

4. IP address of external DNS servers (normally provided by ISP)

Lab 4.2 Installing DNS

4

Objectives

The goal of this lab is to install DNS on your standalone server. After completing this lab, you will be able to:

➤ Install DNS on your standalone server.

Materials Required

This lab will require the following:

➤ Access to *MCSE Guide to Microsoft Windows 2000 Active Directory*

➤ Administrator access to a standalone Windows 2000 server

➤ Windows 2000 Server delivery CD or Network installation files

Activity Prerequisites

The information gathered in the previous lab.

Activity

Use the following steps to install DNS.

1. Log on to the computer using the username (that has administrative rights) and password combination that has been assigned to you.

2. Click **Start**, click **Settings**, and then click **Control Panel**.

3. Double-click **Add/Remove Programs**.

4. Click **Add/Remove Windows Components**.

5. From the available choices, highlight **Networking services** and then click **Details**.

6. From the available choices, click **Domain Name System (DNS)**.

7. Click **OK**, and then click **Next**. Insert the Windows 2000 Server delivery CD or enter the location of the files on the local disk or network share as requested. Then click **OK**.

8. Wait while the system installs the selected components.

9. Click **Finish** and then click **Close**.

10. Close all open dialog boxes. DNS should now be installed.

LAB 4.3 CONFIGURING DNS

Objectives

The goal of this lab is to configure DNS on your standalone server. You will be doing this manually, without using the Wizard, to show the complete steps involved. After completing this lab, you will be able to:

➤ Configure DNS on your standalone server.

➤ Create Forward and Reverse Lookup Zones, configuring other settings as required.

Materials Required

This lab will require the following:

➤ Access to *MCSE Guide to Microsoft Windows 2000 Active Directory*

➤ Administrator access to a standalone Windows 2000 server

Activity Prerequisites

The previous labs in this chapter must be completed.

ACTIVITY

Use the following steps to configure DNS.

1. Log on to the computer using the username (that has administrative rights) and password combination that has been assigned to you.

2. Click **Start**, point to **Programs**, point to **Administrative Tools**, and then click **DNS**.

3. Expand the Local Server, right-click **Forward Lookup Zone**, and then click **New Zone**.

4. In the **New Zone Wizard**, click **Next**.

5. Make sure **Standard primary** is selected and then click **Next**.

6. Type the internal DNS name as defined in Lab 4.1, and then click **Next**.

7. Click **Next** and then click **Finish**. You have now configured DNS with a Forward Lookup zone.

8. Right-click **Reverse Lookup Zone** and click **New Zone**.

9. In the **New Zone Wizard**, click **Next**.

10. Make sure **Standard primary** is selected and then click **Next**.

11. Enter the subnet IP address as defined in Lab 4.1. The address would be set from the subnet and mask used on your internal networks. In this example, an IP subnet of 192.168.0.0 with a mask of 255.255.0.0 is used. Therefore, type **192.168** and leave the rest blank.

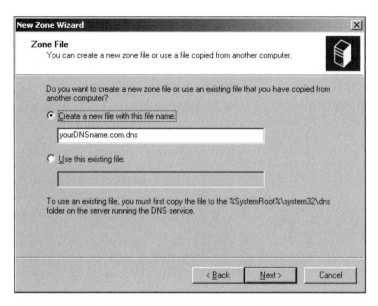

Figure 4-1   The New Zone Wizard for creating a zone file

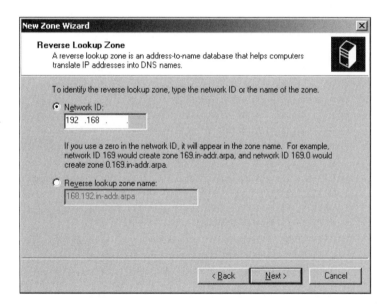

Figure 4-2   Defining the Reverse Lookup Zone using the New Zone Wizard

12. Click **Next**, and click **Next** again, leaving the default settings. Then click **Finish**.

13. You have now configured DNS with a Forward Lookup zone.

14. Right-click your DNS server and click **Properties**.

15. Click the **Forwarders** tab, and check the **Enable forwarders** box.

16. Type the first of the external DNS server addresses supplied by your ISP, and then click **Add** to enter the information.

17. Repeat Step 15 with the second DNS server's IP address.

18. Click **Apply** and then click **OK**. DNS is now configured and operational.

19. Close all open dialog boxes and log off.

LAB 4.4 ADDING RECORDS

Objectives

The goal of this lab is to populate the DNS database with some standard record types. After completing this lab, you will be able to:

➤ Understand the various types and formats of DNS records.

Materials Required

This lab will require the following:

➤ Access to *MCSE Guide to Microsoft Windows 2000 Active Directory*

➤ Administrator access to a standalone Windows 2000 server

Activity Prerequisites

The previous labs in this chapter must be completed.

ACTIVITY

Use the following steps to add new records to the DNS database.

1. Log on to the computer as the administrator, using the password combination that has been assigned to you.

2. Click **Start**, point to **Programs**, point to **Administrative Tools**, and then click **DNS**.

3. Expand the Local Server, expand the **Forward Lookup Zone**, and then expand *YourDNSname*.**com**.

4. Right-click *YourDNSname*.**com** and click **New Host**.

5. Enter the name of your server and then its IP address.

6. Check the **Create associated pointer (PTR) record** option.

7. Click **Add Host** and then click **Done**.

8. Expand the **Reverse Lookup Zone** and then expand the **192.168.*x.x* Subnet**.

9. What do you see?

10. Expand the sub-folder. What do you see now?

11. When you added the standard Host record in Step 5, the Reverse Pointer Record (PTR) and required subnet folder were automatically created. This happened because the Create associated pointer (PTR) record was checked.

12. There are many types of records that can be added; however, the most common will be the standard host record you added earlier.

13. For the Windows 2000 Operating system, most of the records will be added dynamically as clients and services register themselves automatically.

14. Click **Forward Lookup Zones** and right-click *YourDNSname*. Click **Other New Records**.

15. Click the **Host** record. What is its description?

16. Select some other types of records and read their descriptions.

17. Click **Cancel** to return to the DNS console.

18. Close all active dialog boxes and log off.

Lab 4.5 Monitoring a DNS Implementation

Objectives

The goal of this lab is to test and set up monitoring of your DNS implementation using the built-in tool that comes with the DNS service. After completing this lab, you will be able to:

➤ Test and set up monitoring of your DNS implementation.

Materials Required

This lab will require the following:

➤ Access to *MCSE Guide to Microsoft Windows 2000 Active Directory*

➤ Administrator access to a standalone Windows 2000 server

➤ Windows 2000 DNS installed in a previous lab

Activity Prerequisites

The previous labs in this chapter must be completed.

Activity

Use the following steps to test and set up monitoring of your DNS server.

1. Log on to the computer as an administrator.

2. Click **Start**, point to **Programs**, point to **Administrative Tools**, and then click **DNS**.

3. Right-click the local server and click **Properties**.

4. Click the **Monitoring** tab. The options available on this tab allow both manual and scheduled testing of the DNS server.

5. Check **A simple query against this DNS server** and then click **Test Now**. This type of test specifies that the DNS server perform a simple or iterative query. This test is a localized query using the DNS resolver (client) on the server computer to query the local DNS server (also located on the same computer). See Figure 4-3.

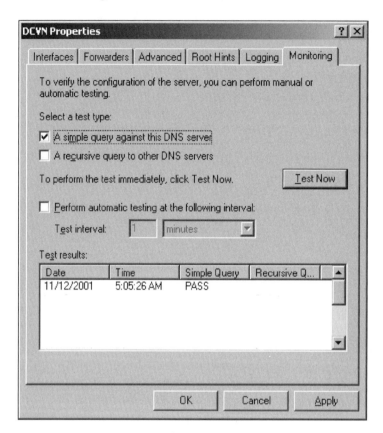

Figure 4-3   Monitoring and testing DNS

6. Clear the A simple query against this DNS server check box and then click **A recursive query to other DNS servers**.

7. Click **Test Now**. This type of test specifies that the DNS server perform a recursive query. This test is similar in its initial query processing to the previous test in that it uses the local DNS resolver (client) to query the local DNS server, also located on the same computer.

By clicking **Perform automatic testing at the following interval**, you can make this test automated. However, the only way to see the results of the test is to have the DNS server monitoring dialog box open, so its value is somewhat limited.

8. Click **Cancel** to return to the main DNS console.

9. Close all open dialog boxes and log off.

LAB 4.6 TROUBLESHOOTING A DNS IMPLEMENTATION

4

Objectives

The goal of this lab is to show some of the methods and tests available to troubleshoot a DNS installation. After completing this lab, you will be able to:

➤ Troubleshoot a DNS service using various tests.

Materials Required

This lab will require the following:

➤ Access to *MCSE Guide to Microsoft Windows 2000 Active Directory*

➤ Administrator access to a standalone Windows 2000 server

➤ Windows 2000 DNS installed as per the previous labs

Activity Prerequisites

The previous labs in this chapter must be completed.

ACTIVITY

Use the following steps to check and troubleshoot your DNS service.

1. Log on to the computer as an administrator.

2. Open a Command Prompt, and type the following (using your Fully Qualified Domain Name—FQDN): **ping *YourSeverName.YourDNSname*.com**

3. You should get four replies from your machine indicating that the FQDN was used to look up the IP address from the DNS server. This would be the first test checking that you can communicate with the machine running DNS. If the ping failed, you would use the machine's IP address to check whether it was working at all on the network.

4. At the Command Prompt, type **nslookup**. See Figure 4-4.

5. If the Reverse Lookup Zone is missing, you should see something similar to Figure 4-5.

6. If only the PTR record for your DNS server was missing, you would see the error: **Non-existent domain**.

7. At the Command Prompt, type **net stop "DNS Server"**.

8. Type **nslookup**. What message or error do you see?

Figure 4-4   Troubleshooting with nslookup

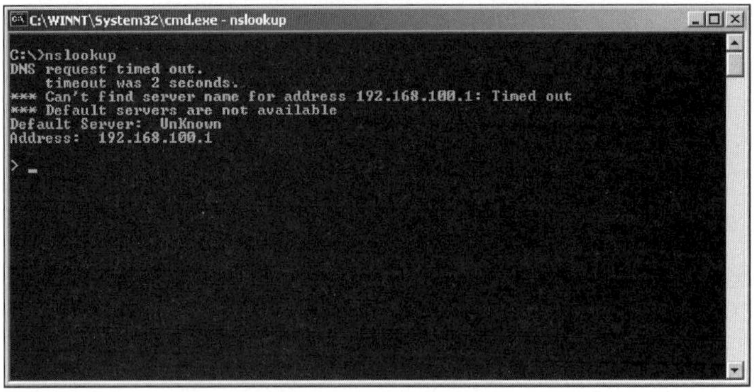

Figure 4-5   Errors shown using nslookup

9. Type **exit** to return to the standard console prompt.

10. Restart your DNS by typing **net start "DNS Server"**.

11. Try pinging a FQDN that is outside of your network, for example www.microsoft.com. This would check whether requests for unknown domain names were being forwarded to external DNS servers.

12. If your DNS server was not able to forward its request properly or the external DNS servers were down, you would get the following error: **Unknown host www.microsoft.com.**

13. Type **nslookup**.

14. Using the external DNS server IP address, type **server extdnsip**, where extdnsip is your external ISP-provided DNS server IP address. This will set the nslookup program to use the external DNS service, rather than your internal service. Try doing a lookup on the www.microsoft.com name again.

15. Type **www.microsoft.com**.

16. If the name is successfully referenced, the external DNS servers are working correctly. This would inidicate that the internal DNS is causing the problem, as you have just checked that the external servers are working and the connection to them is working. The IP addresses you used to configure the DNS server could be entered incorrectly.

17. The tests that were carried out in the previous lab would also have indicated a problem.

4

18. Sometimes a problem with DNS could be caused by an older record being held in either the local database or the cache that contains externally referenced information. The first problem can be resolved by updating the incorrect record; the second problem would resolve itself in time since the entries that are cached have a limited lifetime. After a set period, they would be updated from the external DNS servers.

19. If the problem needs immediate resolution, you can flush the cache. Right-click your server and click **Clear cache**. This would delete all of the records held in the DNS server's cache.

20. Close all active dialog boxes and log off.

INSTALLING ACTIVE DIRECTORY

Labs included in this chapter

➤ Lab 5.1 Creating a New Domain Using DC Promo

➤ Lab 5.2 Checking Active Directory DNS

➤ Lab 5.3 Adding a Second Server to the Domain

➤ Lab 5.4 Promoting a New Member Server to a DC

➤ Lab 5.5 Changing the Domain Mode

➤ Lab 5.6 Demoting a DC

Microsoft MCSE Exam #70-217 Objectives	
Objective	**Lab**
Installing and Configuring Active Directory	5.1, 5.2, 5.3, 5.4, 5.5, 5.6
Installing, Configuring, Managing, Monitoring, and Troubleshooting DNS for Active Directory	5.2
Managing, Monitoring, and Optimizing the Components of Active Directory	5.1, 5.2, 5.3, 5.4, 5.5, 5.6
Configuring, Managing, Monitoring, and Troubleshooting Security in a Directory Services Infrastructure	5.1, 5.2, 5.3, 5.4, 5.5, 5.6

LAB SCENARIO

The Labs in this chapter relate to the creation of domains and the setup of AD—creating a domain, adding to the domain, and finally removing a domain controller from the domain.

LAB 5.1 CREATING A NEW DOMAIN USING DC PROMO

Objectives

The goal of this lab is to demonstrate domain creation using the Windows 2000 server DC Promo wizard. You will become familiar with the process involved and use some of the information from the previous chapters. After completing this lab, you will be able to:

➤ Create a domain using Windows 2000 DC Promo wizard.

➤ Install Active Directory.

Materials Required

This lab will require the following:

➤ Access to *MCSE Guide to Microsoft Windows 2000 Active Directory*

➤ Administrator access to a standalone Windows 2000 server

Activity Prerequisites

Chapter 4 labs must be completed. The machine's IP setting for DNS server should be set to use the local machine's DNS service, as the AD install will need to detect the running DNS and use it during the install procedure.

ACTIVITY

Use the following steps to create a new domain and install AD.

1. Log on to the computer as an administrator, using the password combination that has been assigned to you.

2. Click **Start**, click **Run**, and then type **dcpromo**. Click **OK**.

3. In the Active Directory Installation Wizard, click **Next**.

4. Since this machine is going to be the first domain controller in a new domain structure, click **Domain controller for a new domain**, and click **Next**. See Figure 5-1.

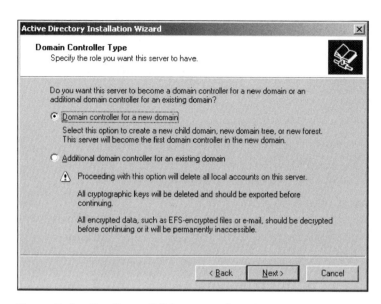

Figure 5-1   Creating a DC in a new domain

> 5. Make sure that the Create a new domain tree option is checked, and then click **Next**. See Figure 5-2.

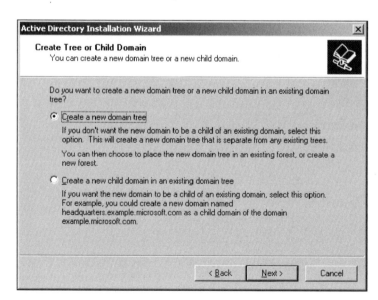

Figure 5-2   Creating a new domain tree

> 6. Make sure that the Create a new forest of domain trees option is checked, and then click **Next**. See Figure 5-3.

Figure 5-3   Creating a new forest

7. Enter your domain name (*YourDNSname*.com) and click **Next**. See Figure 5-4.

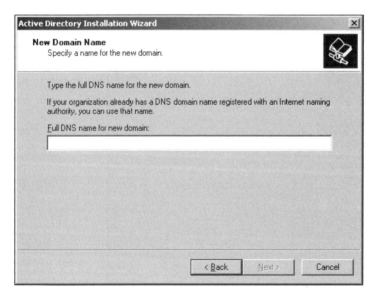

Figure 5-4   Entering the FQDN for the new domain

8. Leave the Domain NetBIOS name set as its default (YourDNSname) and click **Next**.

9. Leave the default Database and Log locations and click **Next**.

10. Leave the default Shared System Volume location and click **Next**.

11. Leave the default security settings and click **Next**.

12. Type the password **password** twice and click **Next** twice. The Active Directory install should now start.

13. When the Active Directory install is completed, click **Finish**.

14. Restart the system when prompted to do so.

 Active Directory is now installed.

5

LAB 5.2 CHECKING ACTIVE DIRECTORY DNS

Objectives

The goal of this lab is to check that the install of Active Directory has correctly added the required entries to the local DNS database. After completing this lab, you will be able to:

➤ Verify that the requried entries have been added to the local DNS database during the AD install.

Materials Required

This lab will require the following:

➤ Access to *MCSE Guide to Microsoft Windows 2000 Active Directory*

➤ Administrator access to a standalone Windows 2000 server

Activity Prerequisites

Chapter 4 labs and Lab 5.1 must be completed.

ACTIVITY

Use the following steps to check that the previous lab correctly added records to the local DNS database.

1. Log on to the computer as an administrator with the password combination that has been assigned to you.

2. Click **Start**, click **Programs,** click **Administrative Tools**, and then click **DNS**.

3. Expand the local server, expand the **Forward Lookup Zone**, and then expand *YourDNSname*.**com**.

4. Now you should be able to see that four new sub-folders have been added. These contain all of the current Active Directory Server services information.

5. Navigate through the sub-directories, and you will see that all of the end node information points to the local server. See Figure 5-5.

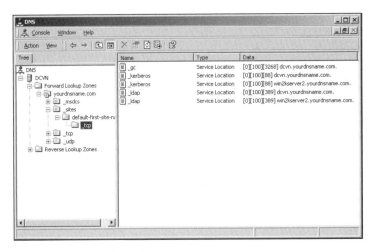

Figure 5-5   Checking the DNS entries

6. If the DNS records are not present, this indicates that something went wrong during the AD install. Use the following steps to add the records manually. If the DNS records are present, close all active dialog boxes and continue.

7. Check that DNS is installed and configured as per the labs of Chapter 4.

8. Stop the DNS service running on the local machine.

9. Using Notepad, open the file **c:\winnt\system32\Config\netlogon.dns**.

10. Open the file **c:\winnt\system32\dns***YourDNSname***.com.dns**.

11. Copy the contents from **netlogon.dns** to the end of *YourDNSname***.com.dns**.

12. Save *YourDNSname***.com.dns** and close both files.

13. Restart the DNS service and go back to Step 2.

LAB 5.3 ADDING A SECOND SERVER TO THE DOMAIN

Objectives

The goal of this lab is to configure a second Windows 2000 Server to be a member server of the new domain. This machine should currently be a standalone server in a default workgroup. After completing this lab, you will be able to:

➤ Configure a second Windows 2000 Server to be a member server of the new domain.

Materials Required

This lab will require the following:

➤ Access to *MCSE Guide to Microsoft Windows 2000 Active Directory*

➤ Administrator access to a standalone Windows 2000 server

Activity Prerequisites

The previous labs must be completed.

ACTIVITY

Use the following steps to configure the new server as a member server of the new domain created in the previous labs.

1. Log on to the computer as an administrator, using the password combination that has been assigned to you.

2. Right-click **My Computer**, and then click **Properties**.

3. Click the **Network Identification** tab, and then click **Properties**.

4. Check the **Member of – Domain** option, and enter the domain name that you created earlier (*YourDNSname*.com).

5. Enter the account name and password that you were using on the previously created domain controller and click **OK**.

6. When you are welcomed to the domain, click **OK** and then click **OK** again.

7. Click **OK** to close the active dialog box and click **Yes** to restart the server.

When the server restarts it will be a member of the new domain.

LAB 5.4 PROMOTING A NEW MEMBER SERVER TO A DC

Objectives

The goal of this lab is demonstrate the process of promoting a domain server from being a member server to being a domain controller in the new domain. After completing this lab, you will be able to:

➤ Promote a domain server from being a member server to being a domain controller in a new domain.

Materials Required

This lab will require the following:

➤ Access to *MCSE Guide to Microsoft Windows 2000 Active Directory*

➤ Administrator access to a member Windows 2000 server

Activity Prerequisites

The previous labs must be completed.

ACTIVITY

Use the following steps to promote the member server to a domain controller.

1. Log on to the computer as an administrator using the password combination that has been assigned to you.

2. Click **Start**, click **Run**, and then type **dcpromo**. Click **OK**.

3. In the Active Directory Installation Wizard, click **Next**.

4. Choose **Additional domain controller for an existing domain**, and then click **Next**. See Figure 5-6.

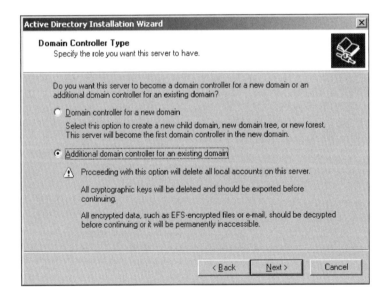

Figure 5-6   Creating an additional DC

5. Enter the credentials used to log on to the Domain Controller during Lab 5-1, and then click **Next**.

6. Leave the default Domain name and click **Next**.

7. Leave the default Database and Log locations and click **Next**.

8. Leave the default Shared System Volume location and click **Next**.

9. Type the password **password** twice and click **Next** twice. The Active Directory configuration should now start.

10. When the Active Directory configuration is complete, click **Finish**.

11. Restart the system when prompted to do so.

12. Log on to the system.

13. Click **Start**, point to **Administrative Tools**, and click **Active Directory Users and Computers**.

14. Expand *YourDNSname***.com**, and expand **Domain Controllers**.

15. You should now see two systems—the first domain controller and the machine you just promoted.

16. Close all dialog boxes and log off.

LAB 5.5 CHANGING THE DOMAIN MODE

Objectives

The goal of this lab is to change the active mode of the domain from mixed to native. Once all DCs in the domain support AD, the change from mixed mode (which supports both Windows 2000 and pre-Windows 2000 domain controllers) to native mode (which supports only Windows 2000 domain controllers) allows the systems to utilize the richer security features available as a result of the Windows 2000 to Windows 2000 connectivity. After completing this lab, you will be able to:

➤ Change the operating mode of the domain from mixed to native.

Materials Required

This lab will require the following:

➤ Access to *MCSE Guide to Microsoft Windows 2000 Active Directory*

➤ Administrator access to a standalone Windows 2000 server

Activity Prerequisites

The previous labs must be completed.

ACTIVITY

Use the following steps to change the operating mode of the domain from mixed to native.

1. Log on to either of the Domain Controllers using the account that has administrative rights.

2. Click **Start**, point to **Programs**, point to **Administrative Tools**, and then click **Active Directory Domains and Trusts**.

3. Right-click the local domain and click **Properties**. See Figure 5-7.

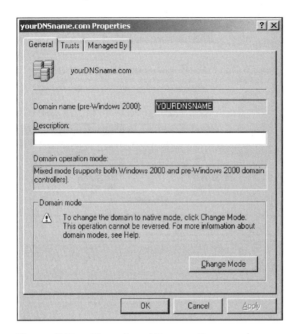

Figure 5-7 Changing AD operating mode

4. Click **Change Mode**, click **Yes**, and then click **OK**.

5. Click **OK** again.

6. After a few minutes, right-click the local domain and click **Properties** again. If the process was successful, the domain operation mode should be the same as shown in Figure 5-8.

7. Close all dialog boxes.

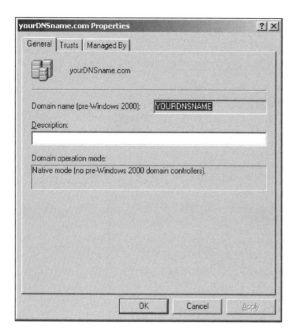

Figure 5-8   AD running in native mode

LAB 5.6 DEMOTING A DC

Objectives

The goal of this lab is to demote a domain controller back to being a member server. After completing this lab, you will be able to:

➤ Demote a domain controller.

Materials Required

This lab will require the following:

➤ Access to *MCSE Guide to Microsoft Windows 2000 Active Directory*

➤ Administrator access to a standalone Windows 2000 server

Activity Prerequisites

The previous labs must be completed.

ACTIVITY

Use the following steps to demote the previously promoted server back to being a member server.

1. Click **Start**, click **Run**, and then type **dcpromo**. Click **OK**.

2. In the Active Directory Installation Wizard, click **Next**.

3. Make sure that the check box for This is the last domain controller in the domain is cleared, and then click **Next**. See Figure 5-9.

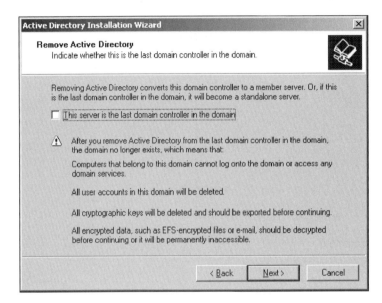

Figure 5-9   Removing a DC from the domain

4. Type the password **password** twice and click **Next** twice. The Active Directory configuration should now start.

5. When the Active Directory removal is complete, click **Finish**.

6. Restart the system when prompted to do so.

7. Log on to the first domain controller with the account that you have been using.

8. Click **Start**, point to **Administrative Tools**, and click **Active Directory Users and Computers**.

9. Expand *YourDNSname*.**com**, and expand **Domain Controllers**.

10. You should now see one system, the first domain controller.

11. Close all dialog boxes and log off.

CHAPTER SIX

ACTIVE DIRECTORY CONFIGURATION

Labs included in this chapter

➤ Lab 6.1 Creating Sites

➤ Lab 6.2 Creating Subnets

➤ Lab 6.3 Creating Site Links

➤ Lab 6.4 Moving Objects

➤ Lab 6.5 Looking at DC Roles

➤ Lab 6.6 Adding a New GC Server

➤ Lab 6.7 Creating Organizational Units

Microsoft MCSE Exam #70-217 Objectives	
Objective	Lab
Installing and Configuring Active Directory	6.1, 6.2, 6.3, 6.4, 6.5, 6.6, 6.7
Configuring, Managing, Monitoring, Optimizing, and Troubleshooting Change and Configuration Management	6.1, 6.2, 6.4, 6.7
Managing, Monitoring, and Optimizing the Components of Active Directory	6.4, 6.5, 6.6
Configuring, Managing, Monitoring, and Troubleshooting Security in a Directory Services Infrastructure	6.4, 6.5, 6.6

LAB SCENARIO

The labs in this chapter are related to the organization and setup of data communication within Active Directory, and the use of objects and grouping to aid administration. Most of the labs in this chapter will be based around the following scenario. A small builder supplier with its main offices in a suburb of Chicago has just opened a new office and store in Springfield (two hours away from Chicago).

They have a Windows 2000 domain running AD and want to expand this to cover a new network infrastructure being set up for the Springfield office. Most of the administration will take place from the main office. The link between the two sites is through the Internet utilizing a VPN with limited bandwidth.

LAB 6.1 CREATING SITES

Objectives

The goal of this lab is to configure AD with the information required to define a new site. In the following labs, this will be the basis for creating a specific connection between Chicago and Springfield for AD communications. After completing this lab, you will be able to:

➤ Understand the information needed for defining a new site.

➤ Configure AD so that you can define a new site.

Materials Required

This lab will require the following:

➤ Administrator access to the Windows 2000 AD domain created in previous labs

➤ Access to *MCSE Guide to Microsoft Windows 2000 Active Directory*

Activity Prerequisites

A Windows 2000 Active Directory Domain configured as per the previous labs.

ACTIVITY

Use the following steps to create a new site within AD.

1. Log on to the domain controller as an administrator, using the password combination that has been assigned to you.

2. Click **Start**, point to **Programs**, point to **Administrative Tools**, and then click **Active Directory Sites and Services**.

3. Right-click **Sites** and click **New Site**.

4. Type **Springfield** for the Name, choose the **DEFAULTIPSITELINK**, and click **OK**. A dialog box will open as shown in Figure 6-1.

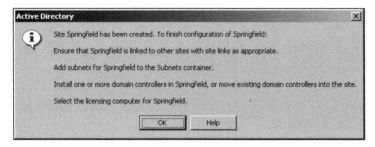

Figure 6-1   Informational message after new site creation

5. Click **OK**.

6. Expand **Sites**, expand **Inter–Site Transports**, and then expand **IP**. The AD Sites and Services dialog box opens. See Figure 6-2.

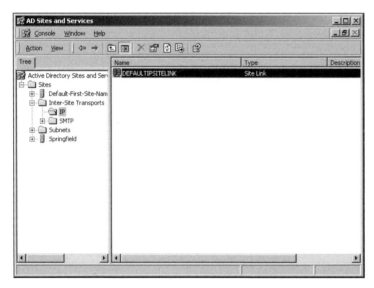

Figure 6-2   Accessing the default site link

7. Right-click **DEFAULTIPSITELINK** and click **Properties**. The DEFAULTIPSITELINK Properties dialog box opens, as shown in Figure 6-3. The General tab indicates that the Default-First-Site-Name and the Springfield sites are connected using the default IP site link that was installed when AD was configured.

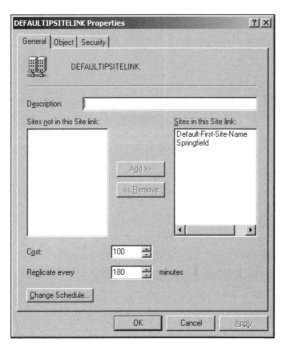

Figure 6-3 DEFAULTIPSITELINK properties

8. Click **OK** to return to the AD Sites and Services dialog box.

9. Close all dialog boxes.

LAB 6.2 CREATING SUBNETS

Objectives

The goal of this lab is to configure AD with the information required to define a new subnet. This will also be required in the following labs. After completing this lab, you will be able to:

➤ Understand the information needed for defining a new subnet.

➤ Configure AD so that you can define a new subnet.

Materials Required

This lab will require the following:

➤ Administrator access to a Windows 2000 server

➤ Access to *MCSE Guide to Microsoft Windows 2000 Active Directory*

Activity Prerequisites

The previous lab must be completed successfully.

ACTIVITY

6

Use the following steps to ensure that the previous lab correctly added records to the local DNS database.

1. Click **Start**, point to **Programs**, point to **Administrative Tools**, and then click **Active Directory Sites and Services**.

2. Expand **Sites** and then expand **Subnets**. Right-click **Subnets** and choose **New Subnet**.

3. Enter **192.168.101.0** as the Address and **255.255.255.0** as the Mask.

4. Click the **Springfield** site object and click **OK**. See Figure 6-4.

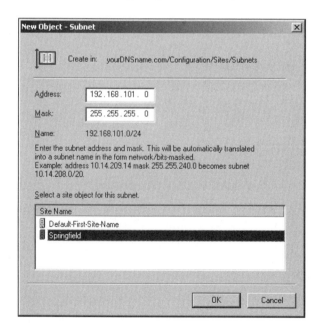

Figure 6-4   Ceating a new subnet

5. Close all dialog boxes.

LAB 6.3 CREATING SITE LINKS

Objectives

The goal of this lab is to create a new site link between the two sites/subnets that define the two offices. This will conserve network bandwidth by regulating replication schedules and compressing data. After completing this lab, you will be able to:

➤ Create a new site link.

➤ Configure the new site link.

Materials Required

This lab will require the following:

➤ Administrator access to a Windows 2000 server

➤ Access to *MCSE Guide to Microsoft Windows 2000 Active Directory*

Activity Prerequisites

The previous labs must be completed.

ACTIVITY

Use the following steps to create a new site link and configure it to be used by the new site/subnet for Springfield.

1. Click **Start**, point to **Programs**, point to **Administrative Tools**, and then click **Active Directory Sites and Services**.

2. Expand **Sites**, expand **Inter-Site Transports**, and right-click **IP**. Then click **New Site Link**.

3. Type **Chicago-Springfield replication connection** for the Name and click **OK**.

4. Right-click the new connection and click **Properties**.

5. You should now see a dialog box configured like the one in Figure 6-5.

6. The knowledge consistency checker (KCC) uses this information to create Active Directory connections.

7. Click **OK** to return to the main dialog box.

8. Close all dialog boxes and log off.

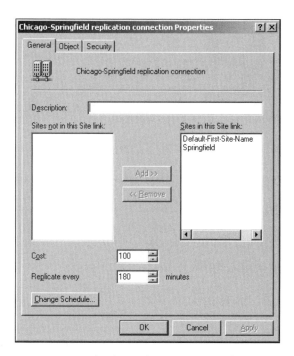

Figure 6-5   Checking the properties of a new site link

LAB 6.4 MOVING OBJECTS

Objectives

The goal of this lab is to demonstrate the ease of moving objects within AD. As part of the scenario, a new DC will be required for the Springfield office. You will create a new domain controller and then move it within AD to the remote site that has been created previously. After completing this lab, you will be able to:

➤ Move objects within AD.

➤ Move objects within AD to a remote site.

Materials Required

This lab will require the following:

➤ Access to *MCSE Guide to Microsoft Windows 2000 Active Directory*

➤ Administrative access to the domain controller

➤ Administrative access to a member server

Activity Prerequisites

The previous labs must be completed.

ACTIVITY

Use the following steps to promote the member server to become a domain controller.

1. Log on to the member server as an administrator, using the password combination that has been assigned to you.

2. Click **Start**, click **Run**, and then type **dcpromo**. Click **OK**.

3. In the Active Directory Installation Wizard, click **Next**.

4. Choose **Additional domain controller for an existing domain**, and then click **Next**.

5. Enter the administrative credentials from the domain controller, and then click **Next**.

6. Leave the default Domain name and click **Next**.

7. Leave the default Database and Log locations and click **Next**.

8. Leave the default Shared System Volume location and click **Next**.

9. Type the password **password** twice, and then click **Next** twice.

10. When the Active Directory installation is complete, click **Finish**.

11. Restart the system when prompted to do so.

12. Once the server has restarted, log on again as an administrator.

13. Click **Start**, point to **Programs**, point to **Administrative Tools**, and then click **Active Directory Sites and Services**.

14. Expand **Sites**, expand **Default-First-Site-Name**, and then expand **Servers**.

15. Right-click your new domain controller and click **Move**.

16. In the Move Server dialog box shown in Figure 6-6, click **Springfield** and then click **OK**. Now the new domain controller is physically moved to the Springfield location and its IP address is changed to work on the new subnet.

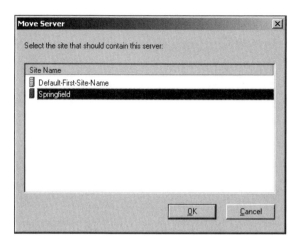

Figure 6-6   Moving a server to another site

 If the KCC does not create an AD connector, you will need to create one manually.

17. Close the active dialog box and log off.

LAB 6.5 LOOKING AT DC ROLES

Objectives

The goal of this lab is to locate the information showing the AD roles of DCs within the domain and the methods used to alter the roles of specified servers. There are six roles. The first is the Global Catalog, which is covered in the next lab; the other five are specific to a single server in a forest. These are called Operation masters. There is a graphical method and a command line utility method for changing server roles. This lab provides an example of each. After completing this lab, you will be able to:

➤ Locate information showing the AD roles of domain controllers.

➤ Alter the roles of specified servers using graphical and command line utility methods.

Materials Required

This lab will require the following:

➤ Administrator access to a Windows 2000 server

➤ Access to *MCSE Guide to Microsoft Windows 2000 Active Directory*

Activity Prerequisites

The previous labs must be completed.

ACTIVITY

Use the following steps to access three of the server roles, RID, PDC, and Infrastructure, as required under AD.

1. Log on to either domain controller as an administrator using the password combination that has been assigned to you.

2. Click **Start**, point to **Programs**, point to **Administrative Tools**, and then click **Active Directory Users and Computers**.

3. In the now active dialog box, right-click *YourDNSname*.com and click **Operations Masters**.

4. The Operations Master dialog box opens, as shown in Figure 6-7. This utility allows you to change three of the five Operation roles.

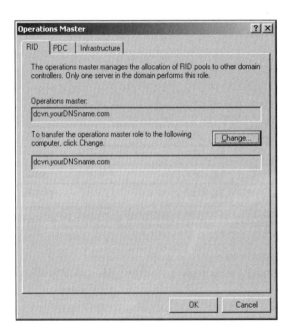

Figure 6-7   Changing server roles

5. Do not make any changes. Click **OK** to close the Operations Master dialog box.

6. Close all dialog boxes.

ACTIVITY

Use the following steps to run the ntdsutil command, which is the utility used to modify and control the many service roles required under AD.

1. Click **Start**, click **Run**, type **cmd**, and then press **Enter**.

2. At the Command Prompt, type **ntdsutil**.

3. At the ntdsutil prompt, type **roles**.

4. At the fsmo maintenance prompt, type **connections**.

5. At the server connections prompt, type **connect to server**, followed by the fully qualified domain name.

6. At the server connections prompt, type **quit**.

7. At the fsmo maintenance prompt, type **?**. See Figure 6-8.

6

```
C:\WINNT\System32\cmd.exe - ntdsutil                                    _|□|×|
Binding to dcvn.yourdnsname.com ...
Connected to dcvn.yourdnsname.com using credentials of locally logged on user
server connections: quit
fsmo maintenance: ?
?                              - Print this help information
Connections                    - Connect to a specific domain controller
Help                           - Print this help information
Quit                           - Return to the prior menu
Seize domain naming master     - Overwrite domain role on connected server
Seize infrastructure master    - Overwrite infrastructure role on connected serv
er
Seize PDC                      - Overwrite PDC role on connected server
Seize RID master               - Overwrite RID role on connected server
Seize schema master            - Overwrite schema role on connected server
Select operation target        - Select sites, servers, domains, roles and Namin
g Contexts
Transfer domain naming master  - Make connected server the domain naming master
Transfer infrastructure master - Make connected server the infrastructure maste
r
Transfer PDC                   - Make connected server the PDC
Transfer RID master            - Make connected server the RID master
Transfer schema master         - Make connected server the schema master

fsmo maintenance:
```

Figure 6-8   The ntdsutil command

8. This now gives you access to the commands to alter the services available from specific servers on the domain.

9. Type **Quit**, type **Quit** again, and then type **Exit**.

10. Close all dialog boxes and log off.

LAB 6.6 ADDING A NEW GC SERVER

Objectives

The goal of this lab is to add a new Global Catalog server. This is the only server role that is used on more than one server in a forest. After completing this lab, you will be able to:

➤ Add a new Global Catalog server.

Materials Required

This lab will require the following:

➤ Administrator access to a Windows 2000 server

➤ Access to *MCSE Guide to Microsoft Windows 2000 Active Directory*

Activity Prerequisites

The previous labs must be completed.

ACTIVITY

Use the following steps to create a new Global Catalog server.

1. Log on to either domain controller as an administrator using the password combination that has been assigned to you.

2. Click **Start**, point to **Programs**, point to **Administrative Tools**, and then click **Active Directory Sites and Services**.

3. Expand **Sites**, expand **Springfield**, and then click the new domain controller.

4. Right-click **NTDS Settings** and click **Properties**.

5. Click the **Global Catalog** check box and click **OK**. See Figure 6-9.

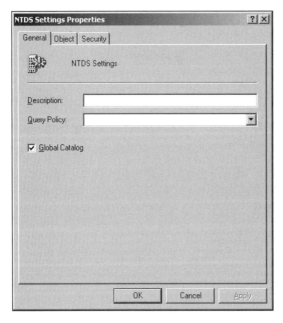

Figure 6-9   Creating a new GC

6. Close all dialog boxes and log off.

LAB 6.7 CREATING ORGANIZATIONAL UNITS

Objectives

The goal of this lab is to create new Organizational Units (OUs) within Active Directory. After completing this lab, you will be able to:

➤ Create a new OU within AD.

Materials Required

This lab will require the following:

➤ Administrator access to a Windows 2000 server

➤ Access to *MCSE Guide to Microsoft Windows 2000 Active Directory*

Activity Prerequisites

The previous labs must be completed.

ACTIVITY

Use the following steps to create an OU in the current domain and add a user account to it.

1. Log on to either domain controller as an administrator using the password combination that has been assigned to you.

2. Click **Start**, point to **Programs**, point to **Administrative Tools**, and then click **Active Directory Users and Computers**.

3. Right-click *YourDNSname*.**com** and click **New − Organizational Unit**.

4. Type in a name for the new OU and click **OK**.

5. Right-click the new OU and click **New − User**.

6. Type the required detail to create a test account, and click **Next**. See Figure 6-10.

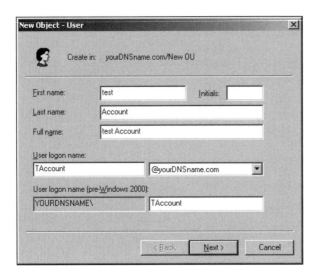

Figure 6-10   Creating a test user account

7. Enter a password twice and click **Next**, and then click **Finish**. You have now created a new OU and populated it with a new user account.

8. Close all dialog boxes and log off.

CHAPTER SEVEN

AD ADMINISTRATION

Labs included in this chapter

➤ Lab 7.1 Searching for Specifics
➤ Lab 7.2 Publishing Shared Folders
➤ Lab 7.3 User Access and Security
➤ Lab 7.4 Inheritable Permissions
➤ Lab 7.5 Delegating Control
➤ Lab 7.6 Moving Objects Within a Domain
➤ Lab 7.7 Moving Objects Between Domains

Microsoft MCSE Exam #70-217 Objectives	
Objective	Lab
Installing and Configuring Active Directory	7.3
Configuring, Managing, Monitoring, Optimizing, and Troubleshooting Change and Configuration Management	7.4, 7.5, 7.6, 7.7
Managing, Monitoring, and Optimizing the Components of Active Directory	7.1, 7.2, 7.3, 7.4, 7.5, 7.6, 7.7
Configuring, Managing, Monitoring, and Troubleshooting Security in a Directory Services Infrastructure	7.4, 7.5

LAB SCENARIO

The Labs in this chapter are designed to show methods for access and administration of Active Directory. The student will create two local printers and have them listed in the Active Directory, and then search for them by specified criteria.

LAB 7.1 SEARCHING FOR SPECIFICS

Objectives

The goal of this lab is to demonstrate some search methods that are available when using Windows 2000 and Active Directory. After completing this lab, you will be able to:

➤ Add a printer.

➤ Set printer sharing and list a printer in AD.

➤ Search for a printer.

Materials Required

This lab will require the following:

➤ Access to *MCSE Guide to Microsoft Windows 2000 Active Directory*

➤ Administrator access to a Windows 2000 server AD domain

Activity Prerequisites

This lab requires access to a Windows 2000 AD domain.

ACTIVITY

Use the following steps to add a printer, set sharing for a printer, and search for a printer.

1. Log on to the computer as an administrator, using the password combination that has been assigned to you.

2. Click **Start**, point to **Settings**, and then click **Printers**.

3. Double-click **Add Printer**.

4. Click **Next** and choose **Local Printer.** Clear the auto detect option and click **Next**.

5. Click **LPT1** and click **Next**.

6. Choose **HP** from the Manufacturers list and choose **HP2000C** from the Printers list.

7. Click **Next**. Type **HPprinter1** as the name and click **Next**.

8. Check **Do not share this printer** and click **Next**.

9. Check **No** to a test page, click **Next**, and then click **Finish**.

10. Repeat steps 3 through 9, selecting a printer of your choice.

11. Right-click **HPprinter1** and click **Properties**. The HPprinter1 Properties dialog box opens, as shown in Figure 7-1.

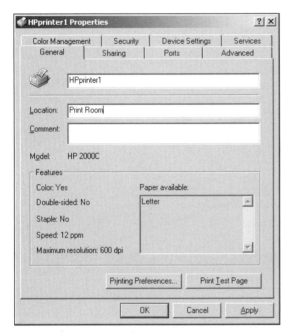

Figure 7-1   Adding location information

12. Type **Print Room** as the location and click the **Sharing** tab.

13. Check the **Shared as** option and type the name **HPprinter1**. See Figure 7-2.

14. Make sure the **List in the Directory** option is checked and then click **OK** to finish.

15. Share and list into AD the other printer you created, modifying or making note of some of its properties.

16. Close the **Printers** folder.

17. Click **Start**, point to **Search**, and click **For Printers**.

18. Enter **Print Room** as the location and click **Find Now**. See Figure 7-3.

19. Clear the search criteria and try searching for the other printer using a known parameter from the installation.

20. Close all dialog boxes. Click **Start**, point to **Programs**, point to **Administrative Tools**, and then click **Active Directory Users and Computers**.

21. Right-click *YourDNSname*.com and click **Find**.

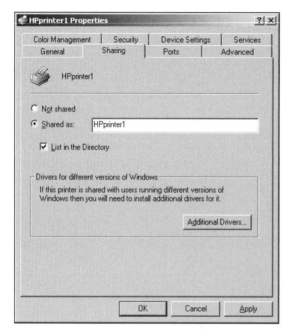

Figure 7-2   Listing the printer in AD

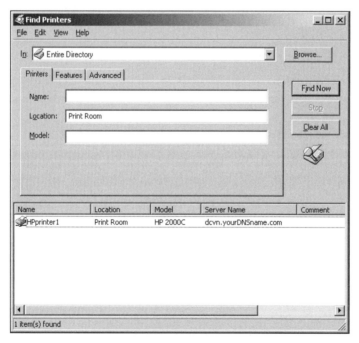

Figure 7-3   Finding the printer by location

22. From the **Find** pull–down list, click **Printers**.

23. Click the **Features** tab. See Figure 7-4.

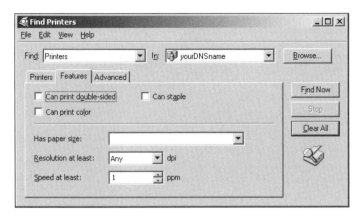

Figure 7-4   Search criteria

24. Check the option **Can print color** and, from the Has paper size pull-down list, choose **Letter**.

25. Click **Find Now**. This is a multi criteria search within Active Directory. See the results in Figure 7-5.

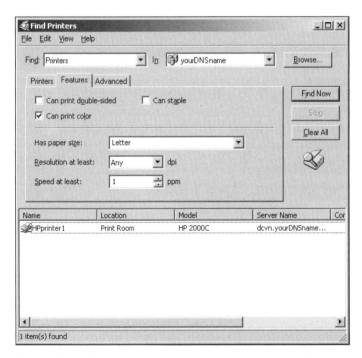

Figure 7-5   Finding a printer by paper size and printing capabilities

26. Close all dialog boxes and log off.

LAB 7.2 PUBLISHING SHARED FOLDERS

Objectives

The goal of this lab is to demonstrate the methods available to publish a shared folder in AD, allowing it be searched for. After completing this lab, you will be able to:

> ➤ Publish a shared folder in AD.

> ➤ Allow the folder to be searched for.

Materials Required

This lab will require the following:

> ➤ Access to *MCSE Guide to Microsoft Windows 2000 Active Directory*

> ➤ Administrator access to a Windows 2000 server AD domain

Activity Prerequisites

This lab requires access to a Windows 2000 AD domain.

ACTIVITY

Use the following steps to share a directory, publish it in Active Directory, and then search for it based upon specific keywords.

1. Log on to the computer as an administrator, using the password combination that has been assigned to you.

2. Create a new folder on drive C: called **Published** and share it using the same name.

3. Click **Start**, point to **Programs**, point to **Administrative Tools**, and click **Active Directory Users and Computers**.

4. Expand *YourDNSname*.com, right-click the OU you created in Lab 7 of Chapter 6, and click **New – Shared Folder**.

5. Type **Published directory** as the Name and **\\dcvn\published** as the Network path. See Figure 7-6.

6. Click **OK** to finish.

7. Right-click the new **Published Directory** and click **Properties**.

8. Enter a description and then click **Keywords**.

9. Type **Lab 7** and then click **Add**. Type **Test folder** and then click **Add**. See Figure 7-7.

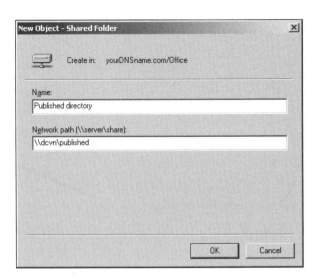

Figure 7-6   Listing a shared folder in AD

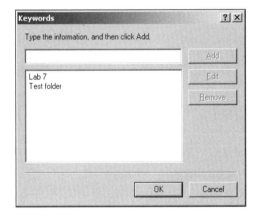

Figure 7-7   Adding keywords to published folders

10. Click **OK** twice to finish and return to the Active Directory Users and Computers dialog box.

11. Right-click *YourDNSname*.**com** and click **Find**.

12. From the Find pull-down list, choose **Shared Folders**.

13. Type **Lab 7** in Keywords and then click **Find Now**. See Figure 7-8.

14. Close all dialog boxes and log off.

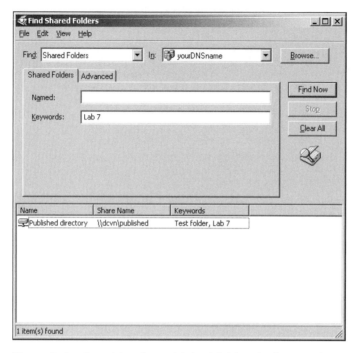

Figure 7-8   Searching for published folders by keywords

Lab 7.3 User Access and Security

Objectives

The goal of this lab is to examine the underlying security of objects. This example demonstrates how file security is achieved by controlling access to a new directory tree. After completing this lab, you will be able to:

➤ Create a new directory tree.

➤ Control access permission to the tree.

Materials Required

This lab will require the following:

➤ Access to *MCSE Guide to Microsoft Windows 2000 Active Directory*

➤ Administrator access to a Windows 2000 server

Activity Prerequisites

There are no prerequisites other than administrator access to an NTFS disk.

ACTIVITY

Use the following steps to create a new directory tree and control the access permission to it.

1. Log on to the computer as an administrator, using the password combination that has been assigned to you.

2. Open **My Computer** and then open your C: drive.

3. Right-click a blank space within the dialog box and choose **New – Folder**.

4. Type the name **Folder 1** and then open the new folder.

5. Right-click a blank space within the dialog box and choose **New – Folder**.

6. Type the name **Folder 2**.

7. Navigate back to C:, right-click **Folder 1**, click **Properties**, and then click the **Security** tab.

8. What permissions are set for this folder?

9. Click **Advanced** and then click **Add**.

10. Choose **Authenticated Users** from the list box and click **OK**.

11. From the Apply onto pull-down list, choose **This folder only**.

12. Click the Deny check box for **Create Files/Write Data**.

13. Click the Deny check box for **Create Folders/Append Data**. See Figure 7-9.

Figure 7-9   Assigning permissions

14. Click **OK** and click **OK** again. Read and accept the notice, and then click **OK** to close.

15. Open **Folder 1** and create a new folder.

16. What happened and why?

17. Open **Folder 2** and try to create a new folder or file in that directory.

18. What happened and why?

19. Close all folders and dialog boxes.

LAB 7.4 INHERITABLE PERMISSIONS

Objectives

The goal of this lab is to show how inheritance works with respect to access rights and permissions. After completing this lab, you will be able to:

➤ Modify the inheritance settings for a folder.

Materials Required

This lab will require the following:

➤ Access to *MCSE Guide to Microsoft Windows 2000 Active Directory*

➤ Administrator access to a member Windows 2000 server

Activity Prerequisites

The successful completion of the previous lab.

ACTIVITY

Use the following steps to modify the inheritance settings for a folder.

1. Open drive C:. Right-click **Folder 1**, click **Properties**, click the **Security** tab, and then click **Advanced**.

2. Highlight the **Authenticated Users Permission Entry** and click **View/Edit**.

3. From the Apply onto pull-down list, choose **This folder, subfolders and files**, and then click **OK**.

4. Check the **Reset permissions on all child objects and enable propagation of inheritable permissions** option, and then click **OK**. See Figure 7-10.

5. Read and accept the notice, and then click **OK** to close.

6. Open **Folder1** and then open **Folder 2**. Create a new file or folder in this directory.

7. What happened and why?

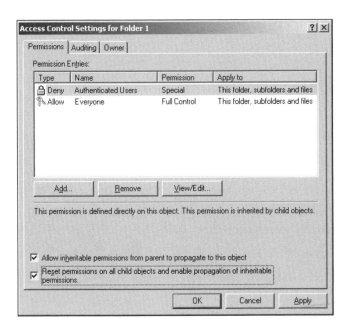

Figure 7-10   Defining Access Control settings

8. Right-click **Folder 2**, click **Properties**, click the **Security** tab, and then click **Advanced**.

9. Uncheck the **Allow inheritable permissions from parent to propagate to this object** option, and then click **Copy** in the notice dialog box.

10. Highlight the **Authenticated Users Permission Entry** and click **Remove**.

11. Click **OK** twice to return to Folder 1. Open **Folder 2** and create a new file or folder in this directory.

12. What happened and why?

13. Close all dialog boxes and log off.

LAB 7.5 DELEGATING CONTROL

Objectives

The goal of this lab is to demonstrate delegation by using the Delegation of Control Wizard. After completing this lab, you will be able to:

➤ Delegate control using the Delegation of Control Wizard.

Materials Required

This lab will require the following:

➤ Access to *MCSE Guide to Microsoft Windows 2000 Active Directory*

➤ Administrator access to a member Windows 2000 server

Activity Prerequisites

The previous labs must be completed.

ACTIVITY

Use the following steps to activate the Delegation of Control Wizard and give a specific user the right to reset passwords for a given OU.

1. Log on to the computer as an administrator, using the password combination that has been assigned to you.

2. Click **Start**, point to **Programs**, point to **Administrative Tools**, and then click **Active Directory Users and Computers**.

3. Right-click the OU you created in the earlier labs, and click **Delegate Control**.

4. Click **Next** and then click **Add**.

5. Choose **Test Account** from the Name list, click **Add**, click **OK**, and then click **Next**.

6. Check **Reset passwords on user accounts** and then click **Next**. See Figure 7-11.

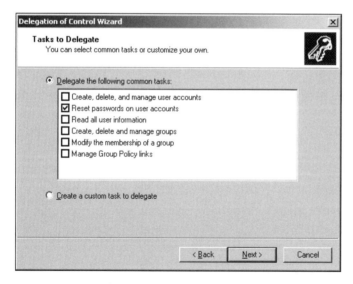

Figure 7-11   Delegating tasks

7. Be sure that the information is correct and then click **Finish**. See Figure 7-12.

8. Create a new test account in the OU, giving it a random password.

9. Close all dialog boxes and log off.

10. Log on to the system as **taccount** with the password of **password**.

Figure 7-12   Completing the Delegation of Control Wizard

11. Click **Start**, point to **Programs**, point to **Administrative Tools**, and click **Active Directory Users and Computers**.

12. Open the test OU, right-click the new test account, and choose **Reset Password**.

13. Change the password to **password** and then click **OK**.

14. Why, as an ordinary user, were you able to reset another person's password?

15. Expand the **Users** folder, right-click the **Administrator** account, and choose **Reset Password**.

16. What happened?

17. Close all dialog boxes and log off.

LAB 7.6 MOVING OBJECTS WITHIN A DOMAIN

Objectives

The goal of this lab is to show the student the process involved in moving objects within the same domain structure. After completing this lab, you will be able to:

➤ Move objects within a domain structure.

Materials Required

This lab will require the following:

➤ Access to *MCSE Guide to Microsoft Windows 2000 Active Directory*

➤ Administrator access to a member Windows 2000 server

Activity Prerequisites

The previous labs must be completed.

ACTIVITY

Use the following steps to move users and other objects to other locations within the same Active Directory domain.

1. Click **Start**, point to **Programs**, point to **Administrative Tools**, and click **Active Directory Users and Computers**.

2. Open the test OU, right-click the test account, and choose **Move**.

3. Click **Users** and then click **OK**. You have now moved a single user account from one OU to another.

4. Right-click **yourDNSname.com** and choose **New – Organizational Unit**.

5. Enter the name **Temp OU** and click **OK**.

6. Expand **Users**, right-click the test account and choose **Move**.

7. Click **Temp OU** and then click **OK**.

8. Right-click **Temp OU** and choose **Move**.

9. Select the test OU and then click **OK**. You have now moved a single OU containing other objects into another OU.

10. Close all dialog boxes and logoff.

LAB 7.7 MOVING OBJECTS BETWEEN DOMAINS

Objectives

This lab is optional. It shows how to load the command line tool MoveTree from the Windows 2000 delivery CD, and outlines its basic usage. This tool is part of the support tools and is loaded using the Windows 2000 Support Tools Wizard. After completing this lab, you will be able to:

➤ Load the command tool MoveTree.

➤ Understand its basic usage.

Materials Required

This lab will require the following:

➤ Access to *MCSE Guide to Microsoft Windows 2000 Active Directory*

➤ Access to the Windows 2000 delivery CD

➤ Administrator access to a member Windows 2000 server

Activity Prerequisites

There are no specific requirements.

ACTIVITY

Use the following steps to install from CD the command line utility **movetree**, and list its many complex functions.

1. Log on to the computer as an administrator, using the password combination that has been assigned to you.

2. From the Windows 2000 Delivery CD, expand the **Support\Tools** directory.

3. Double-click **Setup.exe**, click **Next**, and then enter your name and company details. Click **Next**.

4. Check **Typical**, click **Next** twice, and then click **Finish** when the install has ended.

5. Click **Start**, click **Run**, type **cmd**, and then click **OK**.

6. At the Command Prompt, type **movetree**.

7. The output from this command is shown in Figure 7-13.

```
C:\WINNT\System32\cmd.exe                                        _ □ ×
THE SYNTAX OF THIS COMMAND IS:

MoveTree [/start | /continue | /check] [/s SrcDSA] [/d DstDSA]
         [/sdn SrcDN] [/ddn DstDN] [/u Domain\Username] [/p Password] [/verbose]

  /start        : Start a move tree operation with /check option by default.
                : Instead, you could be able to use /startnocheck to start a mov
e
                : tree operation without any check.
  /continue     : Continue a failed move tree operation.
  /check        : Check the whole tree before actually move any object.
  /s <SrcDSA>   : Source server's fully qualified primary DNS name. Required
  /d <DstDSA>   : Destination server's fully qualified primary DNS name. Require
d
  /sdn <SrcDN>  : Source sub-tree's root DN.
                : Required in Start and Check case. Optional in Continue case
  /ddn <DstDN>  : Destination sub-tree's root DN. RDN plus Destinaton Parent DN.
  Required
  /u <Domain\UserName>  : Domain Name and User Account Name. Optional
  /p <Password> : Password. Optional
  /verbose      : Verbose Mode. Pipe anything onto screen. Optional

EXAMPLES:

  movetree /check /s Server1.Dom1.Com /d Server2.Dom2.Com /sdn OU=foo,DC=Dom1,DC
=Com
          /ddn OU=foo,DC=Dom2,DC=Com /u Dom1\administrator /p *

  movetree /start /s Server1.Dom1.Com /d Server2.Dom2.Com /sdn OU=foo,DC=Dom1,DC
=Com
          /ddn OU=foo,DC=Dom2,DC=Com /u Dom1\administrator /p MySecretPwd

  movetree /startnocheck /s Server1.Dom1.Com /d Server2.Dom2.Com /sdn OU=foo,DC=
Dom1,DC=Com
          /ddn OU=foo,DC=Dom2,DC=Com /u Dom1\administrator /p MySecretPwd

  movetree /continue /s Server1.Dom1.Com /d Server2.Dom2.Com /ddn OU=foo,DC=Dom1
,DC=Com
          /u Dom1\administrator /p * /verbose
```

Figure 7-13   The syntax of cmd.exe

The Active Directory Object Manager (MoveTree) is a command-line tool that allows administrators to move Active Directory objects, such as organizational units and users, between domains in a single forest. These types of operations would be performed to support domain consolidation or organizational restructuring operations, and therefore would not normally be used on a day-to-day basis.

8. Close all dialog boxes and log off.

CHAPTER EIGHT

PERFORMANCE MONITORING

Labs Included in this chapter

➤ Lab 8.1 Using Task Manager

➤ Lab 8.2 Using Performance Monitor

➤ Lab 8.3 Using Event Viewer

➤ Lab 8.4 Working with Log Files

➤ Lab 8.5 Using Alerts

➤ Lab 8.6 Diagnosing Active Directory Performance

Microsoft MCSE Exam #70-217 Objectives	
Objective	Lab
Installing, Configuring, Managing, Monitoring, and Troubleshooting DNS for Active Directory	8.2, 8.3
Configuring, Managing, Monitoring, Optimizing, and Troubleshooting Change and Configuration Management	8.6
Managing, Monitoring, and Optimizing the Components of Active Directory	8.2, 8.3, 8.6
Configuring, Managing, Monitoring, and Troubleshooting Security in a Directory Services Infrastructure	8.2, 8.3, 8.4, 8.6

LAB 8.1 USING TASK MANAGER

Lab Scenario

Now that you have implemented AD in your corporate environment, it is important to understand the tools necessary to collect information, track errors, and gather performance statistics on your AD servers. In this lab, you will be using the Task Manager to check and troubleshoot current performance on a server that seems to be running more slowly than usual.

Objectives

The goal of this lab is to use the advanced features of Task Manager to view current server performance and perform basic diagnostics as necessary. After completing this lab, you will be able to:

➤ Use the various advanced features of Task Manager.

➤ Check processor and memory performance.

➤ Check which processes are using the most resources.

Materials Required

➤ Access to a Windows 2000 Server

➤ Access to *Windows 2000 Server Resource Kit, Supplement 1*

Activity Prerequisites

A copy of the cpustres.exe and leakyapp.exe files can be found on the Windows 2000 Server Resource Kit. Copy the files from either the kit or another location specified by your instructor to a folder on your Windows 2000 system drive.

➤ If necessary, create a folder named **Apps** on your Windows 2000 system drive.

➤ Use My Computer or Windows Explorer to open a window to the Resource Kit folder or the location specified by the instructor.

➤ Copy the following files to the Apps folder: **cpustres.exe** and **leakyapp.exe**.

ACTIVITY

1. To simulate processor utilization, you will use the CPU Stress application.

   a. Use My Computer or Windows Explorer to open a window to your Apps folder. Double-click the **cpustres.exe** application from the Apps folder. A window similar to Figure 8-1 will be displayed.

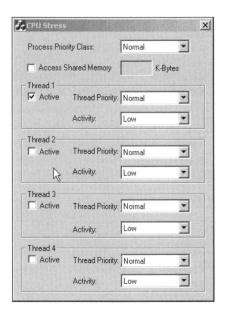

Figure 8-1   The default view of the CPU Stress tool from the Server Resource kit

    b. Start Task Manager by pressing **Ctrl+Alt+Del** and clicking the **Task Manager** button.

    c. Click the **Performance** tab to display a Performance window similar to the one shown in Figure 8-2.

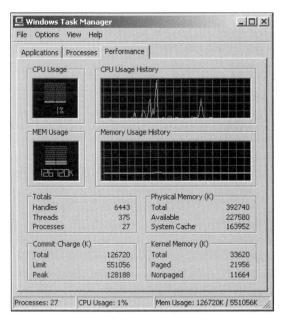

Figure 8-2   The Performance Tab as it appears in Task Manager

    d. Switch to the cpustres.exe application by clicking **CPU Stress** from the Windows 2000 status bar. In the Thread 1 section, change the Activity setting to **Busy**.

    e. Switch to Task Manager by clicking **Windows Task Manager** from the Windows 2000 status bar, and take note of the increase in CPU Usage.

    f. To simulate a stressed server, continue to activate all threads at **medium** activity until CPU Usage regularly exceeds 80 percent. Note the number of medium active threads it takes to bring your CPU Usage to above 80 percent.

    g. Click the **Processes** tab. Determine which process is using the most CPU time by clicking the **CPU** column heading to sort the process list by CPU time.

    h. Close the cpustres.exe software.

2. Another common problem on servers is lack of memory. Having too little RAM for the number of processes running can cause this, or it can be caused by a faulty application that is not releasing memory properly. This second problem is called a memory leak. To simulate an application with a memory leak, you will be using the leakyapp.exe program.

    a. Start the Paint application. Click **Start**, point to **Programs**, point to **Accessories**, and then click the **Paint** icon.

    b. From Paint, choose the **Gone Fishing.bmp** file located in the WINNT folder. Observe how long it takes to load the file. Now load the **Blue Lace 16.bmp** file.

    c. Minimize the **Paint** application.

3. Start the memory leak application.

    a. Use My Computer to browse to the **Apps** folder.

    b. From the Apps folder, double-click **leakyapp.exe**.

    c. To start using up memory, click the **Start Leaking** button as shown in Figure 8-3.

Figure 8-3 The Leaky App application running

4. You will not see a significant slow-down in performance until you have used up all available memory and your system begins to use virtual memory on your hard drive. This process is called generating Page Faults. Switch to Task Manager by clicking **Windows Task Manager** from the Windows 2000 status bar. Then do the following:

    a. Click the **Performance** tab, and note the Total Memory under the Physical Memory section.

b. Observe the MEM Usage window until the value is greater then the Total Physical memory. This may take a few minutes.

5. Activate **Paint** and reload the **Gone Fishing.bmp** graphic file. Note any differences in load time, as compared to when you loaded it previously. Close Paint.

6. To find out what is slowing down the system, switch to Task Manager by clicking **Windows Task Manager** from the Windows 2000 status bar. Then do the following:

   a. Click the **Applications** tab, and note applications and their status.

   b. Click the **Processes** tab and note the application that is using the most memory. (*Hint:* Sort by Mem Usage.)

   c. Add Page Faults and Virtual Memory Size columns to the Processes display:

   - Click the **Select Columns** option from the View menu.
   - Click the **Page Faults** check box.
   - Click the **Virtual Memory Size** check box.
   - Click **OK** to add the selected columns to the Processes tab.

   d. Start the **Paint** application and then switch to the Task Manager.

   e. Note the number of page faults for the **mspaint.exe** process.

   f. Switch to **Paint** and then open the **Gone Fishing.bmp** graphic.

   g. Switch to the **Windows Task Manager** window.

   h. Calculate the number of page faults required by MS Paint to load the Gone Fishing.bmp graphic by subtracting the Initial number of page faults from the number of page faults after loading Gone Fishing.

   i. Close Paint.

7. Exit the leakyapp.exe application, and observe how page faults are affected.

   a. Click the **Processes** tab.

   b. Click the **leakyapp.exe** process.

   c. Click the **End Process** button.

   d. Click **Yes** to terminate the application.

   e. Start the **Paint** application, switch to the **Task Manager** window, and note the number of Initial page faults.

   f. Switch to **Paint** and then open the **Gone Fishing.bmp** graphic.

   g. Switch to **Task Manager**, and recalculate the number of page faults required by MSPAINT to load the Gone Fishing graphic.

8. Close all windows and log off.

LAB 8.2 USING PERFORMANCE MONITOR

Lab Scenario

Task Manager can be used to quickly give you an overview of the performance of a server. In order to get full statistics on all aspects of a server, you will need to use the Performance Monitor Tool. In this lab, you will be using Performance Monitor to check and troubleshoot some of the same issues addressed in Lab 8.1.

Objectives

The goal of this lab is to introduce the various features and capabilities of Performance Monitor, and to check and perform diagnostics on a server. After completing this lab, you will be able to:

➤ Add objects and counters to Performance Monitor.

➤ Use the various views in Performance Monitor.

➤ Connect to a remote server and check performance.

Materials Required

This lab will require the following:

➤ Access to two Windows 2000 Servers

Activity Prerequisites

Lab is to be set up as described in Lab 8.1.

ACTIVITY

1. Click **Start**, point to **Programs**, point to **Administrative Tools**, and then click **Performance** to open the Performance tool similar to the one shown in Figure 8-4.

2. Performance Monitor can be used to view current system activity, or to view activity from a log of past activity. In this step, you identify the options available to monitor and view current system activity with Performance Monitor.

   a. Counters are used to view the activities of system objects. To add a counter to the graph, click the plus sign (+) toolbar icon in the rightmost view pane to display the Add Counters window, as shown in Figure 8.5.

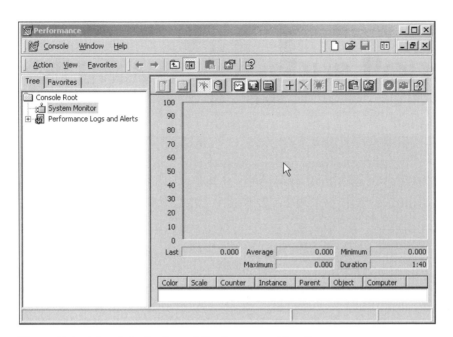

Figure 8-4   The default view of Performance Monitor

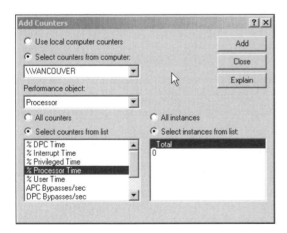

Figure 8-5   The Add Counters tool used to configure Performance Monitor

b. Counters can be added for activities on your computer or on other computers on the network. To add counters for activities on your computer, click the **Use local computer counters** option button.

c. Before selecting the counters, you must identify the performance object you wish to monitor. By default, the **Processor** object is selected first. Each occurrence of the same object is referred to as an instance. Using the Instances options, you can choose to include all instances of the object, a specific object instance, or a Total of the object instances. Verify that the **Total** option is selected.

d. To include all counters for the Processor object, click the **All counters** option button, and click **Add**.

e. To view a specific counter, such as the number of pages/seconds, click the scroll button to the right of the Performance object window, scroll up, and click the **Memory** object.

f. To view just the pages/seconds activity, click the **Select counters from list** option button, and, if necessary, use the scroll bar to scroll down, and then click the **Pages/Sec** counter.

g. Click the **Explain** button to display an explanation of how the pages/sec counter is calculated.

h. Click the **Add** button to add Pages/Sec to the counter list.

i. Click the **Close** button to return to the Performance Monitor graph window.

j. When there are many counters visible, it is difficult to monitor one of the values. The Highlight button allows you to focus on a specific counter. For example, to highlight only the Percent of Processor utilization counter, click the **% Processor Time** counter in the counter window, and then click the **Highlight** button from the tool bar menu. (*Hint:* It looks like a light bulb.) Wait a moment until the % Processor Time is stable, and then move the mouse around. Observe the effect of placing the mouse on processor utilization.

k. Click the **View Histogram** button on the tool bar to view bars representing the relative system usage of each selected counter.

l. Move your mouse around and note two counters that show the highest activity levels on the histogram.

m. Click the **View Report** button on the tool bar, and move the mouse around. Note the counter with the highest value.

n. Click the **View Chart** button to return to Chart view.

o. To clear all counters, click the **New Counter Set** button on the tool bar.

3. Now that you have an overview of Performance Monitor, you will restart the CPU Stress application that was used in Lab 8.1. Before doing so, add the following counters to Performance Monitor.

   ■ Object – Performance, Counter - % Processor Time

   ■ Object – Memory, Counter – Pages/sec

   ■ Object – Memory, Counter – Committed Bytes

4. Start the CPU Stress Application found in the Apps directory. Add low or medium threads to bring your CPU usage to over 80 percent.

5. Switch to the Performance Monitor and observe the Processor Usage and Pages/sec values.

6. To determine the process that is taking the most CPU time, use the process object to add a list of processes to Performance Monitor.

a. Click the **Add** button from the tools bar. Scroll through the Performance Object pull-down box and choose the **Process** object.

b. Ensure that the **% Processor Time** counter is selected and then click **All Instances**.

c. Click the **Add** button and then click Close.

d. Click the **Highlight** button from the tool bar and then click the first Process in the counter list.

e. Use the down arrow key to move through the list and note the process that is taking the most processor time. (*Hint:* Ignore the Idle and Total counters.)

f. To clear all counters, click the **New Counter Set** button on the tool bar.

g. Close the CPU Stress application.

7. To remotely monitor a server, you follow the same procedures, except that you select a remote computer when you add counters.

It is very easy to get mixed up as to which computer you are monitoring. Always note the computer column in the counters section to make sure that you are observing the right server.

a. Click the **Add** button from the tools bar. If necessary, click the **Select counters from computer** radio button. From the pull-down list, choose your partner's computer.

b. Add the objects and counters from Step 3.

c. Ask your partner to start a number of programs and observe the results.

d. When finished, close all programs and return to the desktop.

LAB 8.3 USING EVENT VIEWER

Lab Scenario

The Event Viewer records informational, warning, and failure messages for a variety of operations on your system. It is often your first source in determining the state of the system.

A server has stopped responding to user requests. When you sit down at the server, you are still able to run applications.

Objectives

The goal of this lab is to show how the Event Viewer can be used to check the status of a local or remote server. This information can then be used for general status checking, security information, and troubleshooting. After completing this lab, you will be able to:

➤ Use Event Viewer to monitor and troubleshoot a server.

➤ Use the various filter options on event messages.

➤ Change the size of the Event Logs.

➤ Connect to another server to view event messages.

Materials Required

This lab will require the following:

➤ Access to two Windows 2000 Servers

Activity Prerequisites

Lab is to be set up as stated in the Lab Setup Guide.

ACTIVITY

1. To clear any log entries in the Event Viewer and prepare the server for this lab, do the following.

    a. To Start Event Viewer, click **Start**, point to **Programs**, point to **Administrative Tools**, and then click **Event Viewer**.

    b. Right-click the **Application Log** option and then click **Clear all Events**. A message will be displayed asking whether to save the log. Click **No**.

    c. Repeat Step 1b for all of the other logs.

    d. Close the Event Viewer.

    e. Right-click **My Network Places** and then click **Properties**.

    f. Right-click **Local Area Connection** and then click **Disable**.

    g. Close all windows and restart your system. This will take a little longer because the network card has been disabled.

2. After your system is restarted, log on as administrator and re-open the **Event Viewer**.

3. Click the **System Log** option to display a window similar to Figure 8-6.

4. Double-click the last event message in the rightmost pane. Click the **Up Arrow** and **Down Arrow** buttons on the screen to move through the various messages. Pay special attention to the **Error** type message. Click **OK** to return to the Event Viewer Window.

5. Click the other log files and review the messages generated.

6. As you can see, the failed network card caused the network communication to fail, which in turn caused NetLogon and AD services to fail.

Always look for the root cause of a failure. Repairing the root will usually repair all services above.

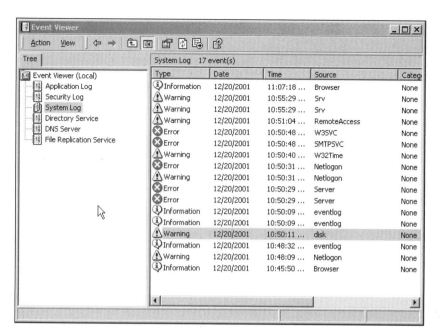

Figure 8-6   The System Log in Event Viewer

7. Often, there are too many messages in an event log. You will now use the filter feature to view a selected group of messages.

   a. Click the **System Log**.

   b. Click the **View** pull-down menu and then click **Filter**. The System Log Properties dialog box opens as shown in Figure 8-7.

   c. Clear all event types except for **Error** and then click **OK**.

   d. Only Error type messages should be displayed.

   e. Click the **View** pull-down menu and then click **Filter**. Reselect all event types and then click the pull-down box from **Event Source**. Scroll down and then click **NetLogon**. Click **OK** to return to the Event Viewer.

   f. Only NetLogon messages should now be displayed.

   g. Click the **View** pull-down menu and click **All Records** to clear the filter.

8. To change the size and characteristics of the Event Logs, do the following.

   a. Right-click any of the Log files and then click **Properties**.

   b. In the Log size section, change the size to **1024K**. Also change the *Overwrite events older than* option to **14** days. Click **OK** to save settings.

9. To view the Event Monitor logs on a remote system, do the following.

   a. Right-click **Event Viewer (Local)** and then click **Connect to another computer**.

   b. Click **Browse** and choose your partner's computer. Click **OK** to open the Event Viewer on the remote system.

   c. Choose the various logs and messages.

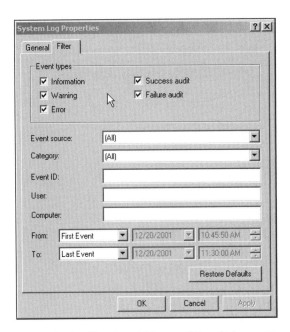

Figure 8-7   The Event Viewer filter dialog settings

10. Close the Event Viewer.

11. To re-activate the network card, right-click **My Network Places** and then click **Properties**. Right-click **Local Area Connection** and click **Enable**.

12. Close all programs and return to the desktop.

LAB 8.4 WORKING WITH LOG FILES

Lab Scenario

In Lab 8.2, you used the Performance Monitor to observe the performance of a server in real time. While this is useful, it is also important to view data over a period of time. This information can then be used for trend analysis, planning, and troubleshooting.

In the past week you have noticed that between 11 am and 1 pm, the server has been responding more slowly than normal. Your task is to log performance during those times for a week and then analyze the results.

Objectives

The goal of this lab is to show the logging capability of Performance Monitor and then use these log files to analyze server performance. After you complete this lab, you will be able to:

➤ Create a log file using Performance Monitor.

➤ Analyze the logged data.

Materials Required

This lab will require no additional material.

Activity Prerequisites

Lab is to be set up as described in Lab 8.1.

ACTIVITY

1. In this step, you will create a log file that will start at 11 am and end at 1 pm. You will need to log Processor, Memory, and Hard Drive usage.

    a. Start the Performance Monitor Tool.

    b. In the left pane, expand the **Performance Logs and Alerts** option and then click **Counter Logs** to display the available logs in the rightmost pane as shown in Figure 8-8.

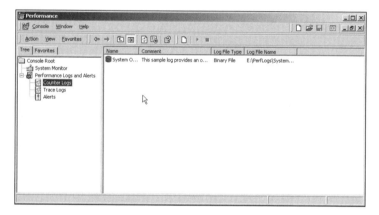

Figure 8-8   Configuring a Performance Monitor Performance Log

    c. Right-click **Counter Logs**, and click the **New Log Settings** option.

    d. Enter **11to1** for your log filename and click **OK** to display the **11to1** window shown in Figure 8-9.

    e. To add counters such as Pages/Sec, click the **Add Counters** button and choose the **Memory** object from Performance objects. Scroll down in the Select Counters list and, if necessary, choose **Pages/Sec**. Click **Add** to add the counter and then click **Close** to return to the 11to1 properties window.

    f. Using Step d from above, add these additional counters.

    - Object – Processor, Counter - % Processor Time

    - Object – Memory, Counter – Committed Bytes

    - Object – Physical Disk, Counter – % Disk Time

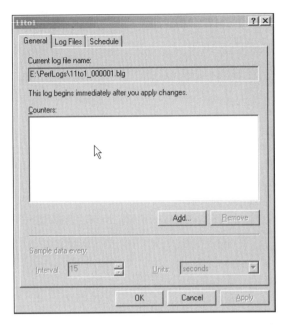

Figure 8-9   The Log Settings Options screen from Performance Monitor

g. When finished, click **Close** to return to the 11to1 properties window.

h. In the Sample Data section, set the interval to every **5** seconds.

i. Click the **Log Files** tab, and note the path to your log file and log file name.

j. Click the **Schedule** tab. A message will be displayed, indicating that the file does not exist. Click **Yes** to create the file.

k. Normally you would set the start and stop time. However, for the purpose of this lab, click **Manually** under the Start Log section.

l. Click **OK** to save your log file settings.

2. Now that you have configured the 11to1 log counters, the next step is to start the log.

a. Right-click your **11to1** log file, and click **Start**.

b. Minimize **Performance Monitor**.

c. Start the CPU Stress application and start two medium threads. Let your system run for a minute or two.

d. Maximize **Performance Monitor**.

e. Right-click your **11to1** log, and click the **Stop** option.

f. Close the CPU Stress application.

3. After the system activity has been logged, you next need to view the 11to1 performance log.

a. In the left tree pane, click **System Monitor**.

b. To view logged data, click the **View Log File Data** button. Navigate to the **<Drive>\PerfLogs** folder and then double-click the name of the 11to1 log file from Step 1i.

c. To add the counters from the log file, click the **Add** button from the tool bar.

d. Click the scroll button to the right of the Performance Object text box. Notice that, because you are viewing the contents of the log file, only the objects and counters you logged are included in object and counter windows.

e. For each performance object listed, click the **All counters** button, and then click **Add**.

f. After all counters are added to the chart, click the **Close** button.

g. From the chart window, click each counter, and note the maximum and minimum values.

4. To view a specific time in the log file, do the following.

a. Click the **Properties** button on the tool bar. Click the **Source** tab to display a window similar to Figure 8-10.

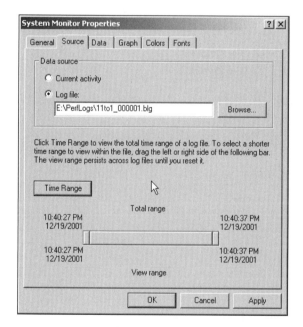

Figure 8-10   Performance Monitor Log file source dialog box

b. Using the mouse, click on the left bar of the View Range section. Drag the bar over to increase the time from the start of the log. Click on the right bar and drag it to decrease the end time of the log. See Figure 8-11.

c. Click **OK** to return to the Chart Window. Notice that the chart now only shows the time range that you selected.

5. Close all programs and return to the desktop.

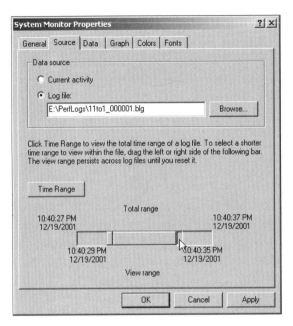

Figure 8-11   Adjusting the time windows for the Performance Monitor Log view

LAB 8.5 USING ALERTS

Lab Scenario

In Lab 8.4, you used a log file to monitor server activity between 11 am and 1 pm. In most troubleshooting situations, you will not have the luxury of knowing exactly when a problem will occur. Alerts give you the ability to trigger messages, trigger other programs, or start a log file, based on an event on your system.

Using the 11-to-1 log files has been useful, but not conclusive. You suspect that there are other times when your server is over-stressed, but you are not sure when. Use Alerts in Performance Monitor to track these times.

Objectives

The goal of this lab is to show how alerts can be used to assist in troubleshooting, as well as in day-to-day maintenance. After completing this lab, you will be able to:

> ➤ Create an Alert that will be triggered by high CPU usage.

> ➤ Modify the Alert to start a log file.

> ➤ View the Alert messages in Event Viewer.

Materials Required

This lab will require the following:

➤ Access to a Windows 2000 Server

Activity Prerequisites

Lab is to be set up as stated in the Lab Setup Guide.

ACTIVITY

1. In this step, you configure Performance Monitor to create an alert based on high CPU usage. Click **Start**, point to **Programs**, point to **Administrative Tools**, and then click **Performance**.

   a. In the left tree pane, expand **Performance Logs and Alerts**, then right-click **Alerts**, and click the **New Alert Settings** option.

   b. Type the name **HighCPU** and click **OK** to display the HighCPU properties window.

   c. Click the **Add** button, and add the **% Processor Time** counter from the **Processor** object. Click **Close** to display a window similar to Figure 8-12.

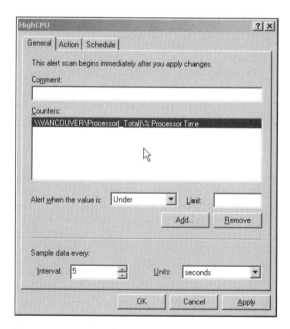

Figure 8-12   Performance Monitor Alert tool configuration view

   d. From the Alert when the value is list box, choose **Over** and in the Limit box, type **90**. Your window should now look like Figure 8-13.

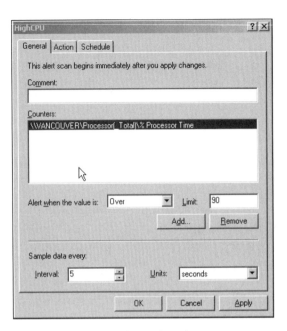

Figure 8-13   A configured Performance Monitor Alert

  e. Now click the Action tab and note the various actions that can be triggered based on this alert. For now, you will only use the default Log an entry in the application event log.

  f. Click the **Schedule** tab, and click the **Manually** start scan option.

  g. Click **OK** to save the alert settings.

2. To start the Alert, right-click the **HighCPU** Alert and click **Start**.

3. Start the Event Viewer. Click **Start**, point to **Programs**, point to **Administrative Tools**, and click **Event Viewer**. Then click the Application Log. There should be one entry from the SysmonLog source, stating that the HighCPU Alert has been started.

4. To stress the CPU, start the CPU stress utility in the Apps folder (cpustres.exe). Activate two or three busy threads to cause your CPU usage to go above 90 percent.

5. Click the Event Viewer button on the status bar and then type **F5** to refresh the screen. Every five seconds, another message should appear. Double-click one of the messages, and note the CPU usage value.

6. Close the Event Viewer and the CPU Stress utility.

7. Return to the Performance Monitor window and right-click the **HighCPU** alert. Click **Stop** to end the alert.

8. You will now use your alert to trigger the counter log that you created in Lab 8.4.

a. Right-click the **HighCPU** alert and click **Properties**.

b. Click the **Action** tab and then click **Start Performance Data Log**. From the pull-down window, select the **11to1** counter log that you created in Lab 8.4. Your window should look similar to Figure 8-14.

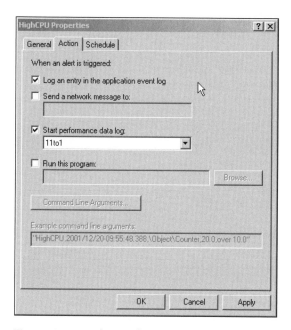

Figure 8-14   The Performance Monitor Data Log configuration view

c. Repeat steps 2 through 4 and then switch to the Performance Monitor window. In the left pane window, click **Counter Logs**. The 11to1 log should have been started.

d. Stop the HighCPU alert first and then stop the 11to1 counter log.

e. Close all programs and return to your desktop.

LAB 8.6 DIAGNOSING ACTIVE DIRECTORY PERFORMANCE

Lab Scenario

Your AD network has been running smoothly for a number of months. Today you have noticed that one of your servers is operating very slowly when your want to view or change anything in AD. You have also received a Global Catalog error when trying to add a new user. However, users have still been able to connect to this server, and access data and applications. It is your job to diagnose this problem and find a solution.

Objectives

During regular AD operation, information is replicated from server to server and site to site. If communication failures occur, AD changes and updates can be delayed, causing inaccurate data and poor server performance. It is important to monitor this traffic on a regular basis for errors as well as performance issues. This lab will use a tool called Replmon.exe which is one of the AD tools available on the Windows 2000 Server CD.

After completing this lab, you will be able to:

➤ Check the status of your AD server using AD Replication Monitor.

➤ Check replication traffic between servers.

➤ Troubleshoot AD errors.

➤ Force replication of AD information.

Materials Required

This lab will require the following:

➤ Access to a Windows 2000 Server with AD installed

➤ Installation of the Windows 2000 Server Support Tools or *Windows 2000 Server Resource Kit, Supplement 1*

ACTIVITY

1. To simulate a connection error with other AD servers, you will need to disable the LAN card on your server.

   a. Right-click **My Network Places** and then click **Properties** to display the Network and Dial-up Connections window.

   b. Right-click **Local Area Connection** and then click **Disable**. This will disable all communications on this network card.

   c. Close the Network and Dial-up Connections window.

2. Click **Start** and then click **Run** to display the Run window.

3. Type **replmon.exe** in the dialog box and then click **OK** to start the Active Directory Replication Monitor. A window should open similar to Figure 8-15.

4. Right-click **Monitored Servers** and then click **Add Monitored Server**.

5. On the Add Monitored Server Wizard page, click the **Search the directory for the server to add** radio button. The name of your domain should automatically be displayed in the dialog box, similar to Figure 8-16.

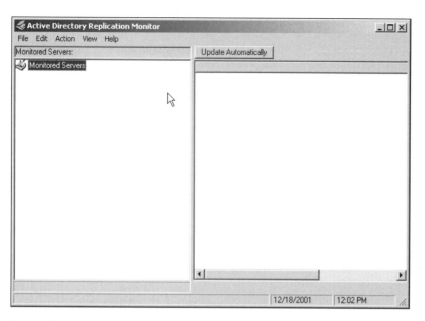

Figure 8-15   Opening the Replication Monitor tool and the initial view

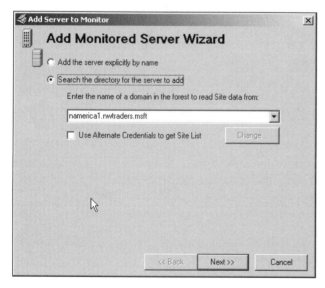

Figure 8-16   Adding a domain controller to Replication Monitor

6. Click **Next** to display the Add Server to Monitor window. Expand **Default–First–Site–Name** and then click the name of your server.

7. Click **Finish** to return to the Active Directory Replication Monitor window. There will be a delay before information about your server is displayed.

8. A window similar to Figure 8-17 should be displayed.

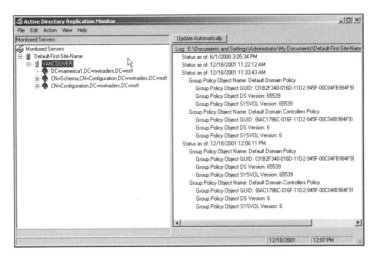

Figure 8-17   The AD replication history in Replication Monitor

9. Expand both the **CN=Schema** and **CN=Configuration** lines in the left pane window. Click on each server listed and note the messages in the rightmost pane. Since the time from when you disabled the network card until the next replication interval has most likely not been reached, you should not see any replication errors.

10. In order to cause the server to start replication before the next interval, you will need to force replication to occur.

   a. Under the CN-Schema entry in the left pane window, right-click the name of your instructor's computer. Then click **Synchronize with this Replication Partner**.

   b. A Source Domain unreachable message should be displayed. Click **OK** to clear the message.

   c. Press **F5** to refresh the screen. A red X should now be displayed on your instructor's computer. See Figure 8-18.

   d. In the right pane, scroll down as necessary to view the error.

11. To generate a status report on the server, do the following.

   a. In the left pane, right-click the name of your server and then click **Generate Status Report**.

   b. When the Save As window opens, select your desktop from the Save In pull-down list, and type **ADErrorReport** in the File Name dialog box. Click **Save** to display the Report Options box.

   c. Click **OK** to generate the report.

   d. Use WordPad to view the contents of the error report on your desktop.

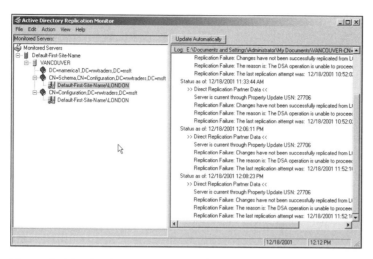

Figure 8-18   Replication Monitor showing information for a specific site

8

12. You have determined the network error and have corrected it. To simulate the repair, reactivate your LAN card.

   a. Right-click **My Network Places** and then click **Properties** to display the Network and Dial-up Connections window.

   b. Right-click **Local Area Connection** and then click **Enable.** This will enable all communications on this network card.

   c. Close the Network and Dial-up Connections window.

13. To force the replication with your instructors' computer, do the following.

   a. Under the **CN-Schema** entry in the left pane, right-click the name of your instructor's computer. Then click **Synchronize with this Replication Partner**.

   b. Press **F5** to refresh the screen. The red X should now be gone.

   c. In the rightmost pane, scroll down as necessary to view the replication information.

14. Close all windows and return to your desktop.

CHAPTER NINE

ACTIVE DIRECTORY MAINTENANCE AND RECOVERY

Labs included in this chapter

➤ Lab 9.1 Extensible Storage Engine

➤ Lab 9.2 The Files of Active Directory

➤ Lab 9.3 Active Directory Dependencies

➤ Lab 9.4 Restoring Active Directory

➤ Lab 9.5 Active Directory Backup

➤ Lab 9.6 Active Directory Maintenance

➤ Lab 9.7 Manual Database Cleanup

➤ Lab 9.8 Basic Backup Principles and Security

➤ Lab 9.9 The Microsoft Backup Utility

Microsoft MCSE Exam #70-217 Objectives	
Objective	**Lab**
Installing and Configuring Active Directory	9.1, 9.2, 9.3, 9.4, 9.5, 9.6, 9.7, 9.8, 9.9
Configuring, Managing, Monitoring, Optimizing, and Troubleshooting Change and Configuration Management	9.4, 9.5
Managing, Monitoring, and Optimizing the Components of Active Directory	9.1, 9.2, 9.3, 9.4, 9.5, 9.6, 9.7, 9.8, 9.9

LAB 9.1 EXTENSIBLE STORAGE ENGINE

Lab Scenario

You have recently implemented AD in your corporate environment and, though it appear
to be working as advertised, you would like to collect more performance information o
the AD database. Specifically, you would like to track performance trends and attempt t
collect data on the size growth of AD. You have previous experience with Performanc
Console, but when you check for the existence of AD Performance Console performanc
objects, you fail to find any such counters. You have searched the *Windows 2000 Serve
Resource Kit, Supplement 1* and found the information you need in an article entitle
"Database Object" located in "Resource Kit Distributed Systems Guide Build # 0050,"
pages 428 to 429. This article details the installation of a dll in the operating system t
enable the collection of Performance Console data. You have the Resource Kit in front o
you and you are ready to begin the installation of this file.

Objectives

The goal of this lab is to install the Performance Console performance object counter
in Performance Console. This is necessary because these counters will be useful for late
data collection as your AD implementation grows in size. After completing this lab, yo
will be able to:

➤ Use Performance Console performance object counters to troubleshoot AD.

➤ Use Performance Console performance object counters to collect diagnostic
  data on AD.

➤ Obtain size estimates on AD.

➤ Make diagnostic estimates of AD database fragmentation levels to apply corrective procedures.

Materials Required

This lab will require the following:

➤ Access to *Windows 2000 Server Resource Kit, Supplement 1*

➤ Access to a Windows 2000 Server with AD installed

Activity Prerequisites

Lab is to be set up as stated in the Lab Setup Guide.

ACTIVITY

Note

This lab requires the use of the Windows 2000 Registry editing tool, regedt32.exe. Do not use the registry editor unless no other method exists to introduce the desired changes.

Caution

Failure to exercise caution when using the registry editor can lead to permanent corruption of the Windows 2000 registry.

1. You will need to search your computer for the file named **esentprf.dll**. When this is located, copy it into a new directory. Name the directory **ESEData** and save it in the C: directory.
2. Click **Start**, click **Run**, and type **regedt32.exe**. Then click **OK**.
3. When Regedt32 opens, check to determine whether the following registry subkeys exist:

    a. HKEY_LOCAL_MACHINE\SYSTEM\CurrentControlSet\Services\ESENT

    b. HKEY_LOCAL_MACHINE\SYSTEM\CurrentControlSet\Services\ESENT\Performance

9

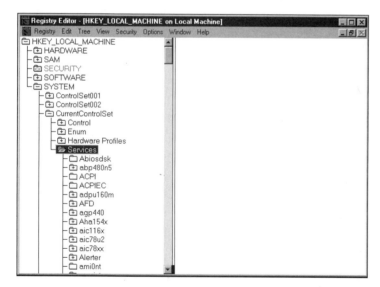

Figure 9-1   Using REGEDT32 to view the Windows 2000 Registry

4. If you did not find these entries in the Registry, you will need to add them.
5. To add these entries to the Registry, perform the following steps.

Caution

Check your spelling before pressing the enter key.

6. You will first need to maximize the HKEY_LOCAL_MACHINE key in Regedt32. After this has been maximized, expand the path: **HKEY_LOCAL_MACHINE\SYSTEM\CurrentControlSet\Services**

7. Double-click the **Services** key. Next, on the Regedt32 menu bar, click **Edit**, click **Add Key**, and, in the Add Key dialog box, type this entry: Key Name: **ESENT**

8. Check your spelling and click **OK**.

9. Move your cursor to the new entry of ESENT and then add the following sub-key using the same process as in Step 7 above. The entry to be added this time is **Performance**. The correct path should be: HKEY_LOCAL_MACHINE\SYSTEM\CurrentControlSet\Services\ESENT\Performance

10. Check your spelling and click **OK**.

11. Move your cursor to the Performance entry. Under the Performance subkey, you will need to add the following entries. Add them one at a time, checking your spelling before clicking **OK**.

    a. Click **Edit**, click **Add Value**, and, in the Value Name field, type the value **Open**. Choose a Data Type of **REG_SZ**, click **OK**, and then, in the String Editor box, enter the value **OpenPerformanceData**. Click **OK** and then add the next value. Make certain to add all values under the path from Step 9 above. Use the table below for the rest of the values.

Table 9-1   ESE performance counter objects

Open	REG_SZ	OpenPerformanceData
Collect	REG_SZ	CollectPerformanceData
Close	REG_SZ	ClosePerformanceData
Library	REG_SZ	C:\esedata\esentprf.dll

12. Locate the file ESENTPRF.INI on your system. When it has been located, copy it to the directory **C:\esedata** and then click **Start**, click **Run**, and then type **cmd**. Then click **OK**.

13. When the Command Prompt opens, type these commands, pressing Enter after each command is typed:

    a. **cd**

    b. **cd\esedata**

    c. **lodctr.exe esentprf.ini**

14. Now you should open Performance Console by clicking **Start**, clicking **Run**, and typing **perfmon**. This will open the Performance Console.

15. Right-click in the Performance Console graph window and choose the **Add Counters** item. Click the down arrow for the box Performance object and search for any instances of **Database**. If you have found some, then you have completed the lab successfully.

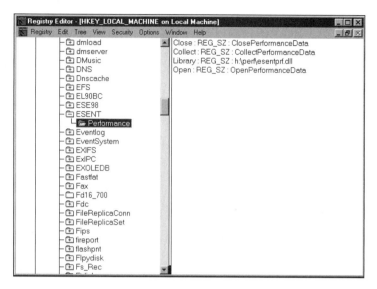

Figure 9-2   Adding the ESENT\Performance entries

9

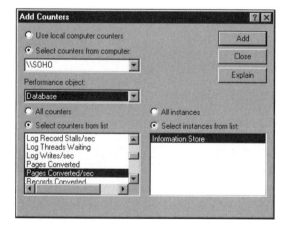

Figure 9-3   The newly added Performance object and counters

LAB 9.2 THE FILES OF ACTIVE DIRECTORY

Lab Scenario

As part of your preparation for the implementation of AD, you need to learn as much as possible about the AD files themselves, such as what they are called and where they are stored on the system. You have just configured your Performance Console to track changes to these files, but you don't know anything else about them yet.

Objectives

The goal of this lab is to locate and identify the database files used by AD. After completing this lab, you will be able to:

➤ Identify the AD database files.

➤ Specify the location of these files.

➤ Understand the purpose of these files.

➤ Understand the use of Performance Console to collect AD data.

Materials Required

This lab will require the following:

➤ Access to *Windows 2000 Server Resource Kit, Supplement 1*

➤ Access to a Windows 2000 Server with AD installed

➤ Performance Console configured from Lab 9.1

Activity Prerequisites

Lab is to be set up as stated in the Lab Setup Guide.

ACTIVITY

1. Your first step will be to locate the AD files themselves. Use the table below and write in the location of the AD files on your server.

Table 9-2   AD Database files

AD Database File Name	File Location
Ntds.dit	
Edb*.log	
Edb.chk	
Res1.log	
Res2.log	

2. After you have located these files, use your new Performance Console functionality to track activity in these files.

3. Open Performance Console by clicking **Start**, clicking **Run**, and then typing **perfmon** at the run line. Press **Enter**. You should see a Performance Console that is very similar to the figure below.

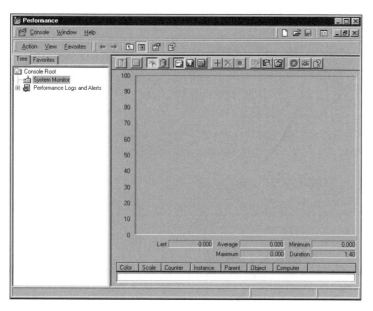

Figure 9-4   The default view of Windows 2000 Performance Console

4. Right-click in the graph pane to bring up a small menu with the Add Counters option on it. Click **Add Counters** and then, from the Performance Object drop-down list, choose two performance objects. First click **Database** as the Performance Object and click **All Counters**. Then click **Add**. Click the Performance object drop-down list again, click the object **Database→ /All Counters**, and also click **All instances** at the same time. Now click **Close** in the Add counters dialog box. Your Performance Console should look similar to the view shown in Figure 9-5.

5. With performance Console now populated, right-click in the Graph pane and click **Properties** to see additional settings. On the System Monitor Properties page, from the View heading, choose each different view in turn to see the format of the data being returned. Note whether any one view is more useful to you than any other. Also note what happens if you change the update time from 1 second to 15 seconds, or even to 1 minute.

9

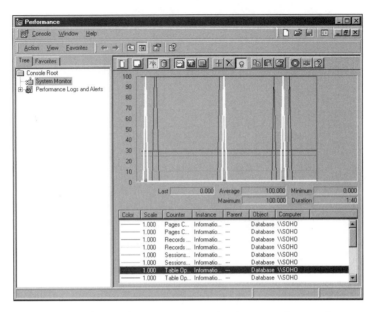

Figure 9-5   The Performance Console showing the newly created objects in place and collecting data

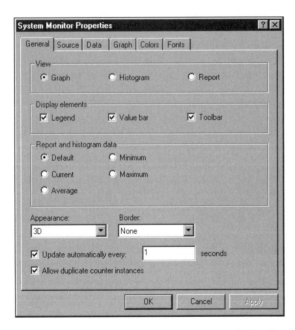

Figure 9-6   System Monitor Properties dialog box showing different configuration settings

6. Trigger some activity in AD to see the results in Performance Console. Note what happens when you add a user in AD. Note whether any of the Performance Console counter objects spike. Continue to explore the impact of accessing the AD database, while watching the activity in Performance Console.

7. When you are finished, close Performance Console.

LAB 9.3 ACTIVE DIRECTORY DEPENDENCIES

Lab Scenario

You are getting closer and closer to your AD implementation. You need to know whether AD has any dependencies, where the dependencies are located, and what they consist of.

Objectives

Remember from your class that the AD dependencies can be broadly considered to be the System State data. You need to know what System State consists of. After completing this lab, you will be able to:

> Identify the individual system components that make up the System State data.

> Know where the System State data is located on a Windows 2000 computer.

> Understand the appropriate rights and permissions to back up the System State data.

Materials Required

This lab will require the following:

> Access to *Windows 2000 Server Resource Kit, Supplement 1*

> Access to a Windows 2000 Server with AD installed

Activity Prerequisites

Lab is to be set up as stated in the Lab Setup Guide.

ACTIVITY

Use the Windows 2000 On-line Help to discover information about the System State components. What exactly do they comprise? Are they specific files, or sections of the operating system? Use the table below to record your results.

Table 9-3

System State Components	Location (if discernable)

LAB 9.4 RESTORING ACTIVE DIRECTORY

Lab Scenario

The unthinkable has just happened. Your AD implementation just crashed. It is 4:30 Monday morning and you still have time before the employees—your users—start to arrive. You need to perform an AD Restore, but what kind of restore do you need to do—a **Nonauthoritative** restore or an **Authoritative** restore? If you remember from class, the Nonauthoritative and the Authoritative restore both start the same way, with the Authoritative restore adding an extra step. Therefore it is in your best interest to perform the Nonauthoritative restore first and then, if conditions warrant, you can perform an Authoritative restore afterwards.

Objectives

The goal of this lab is to give you experience in performing a Nonauthoritative and an Authoritative Restore of AD. You perform part of this lab by booting Windows 2000 into an offline configuration called Active Directory Restore Mode, and then use a command line tool, NTDSUtil.exe, to make the repair of AD. Before you start to use NTDSUtil, it would be prudent to read about the use of this tool in either the Windows 2000 On-line Help guide or the Server Resource kit. After you complete this lab, you will be able to:

> ➤ Differentiate between a Nonauthoritative AD Restore and an Authoritative AD Restore.

> ➤ Use the NTDSUtil tool correctly.

> ➤ Understand the implications of using the NTDSUtil correctly.

> ➤ Understand the implications of using the tool incorrectly.

Materials Required

This lab will require the following:

➤ Access to *Windows 2000 Server Resource Kit, Supplement1*

➤ Access to two Windows 2000 Servers with AD installed

➤ Server1

➤ Server2

Activity Prerequisites

Lab is to be set up as stated in the Lab Setup Guide.

ACTIVITY

1. The first step in this lab is to synchronize your domain controller with your partner's domain controller. You do this by opening the Active Directory Sites and Services tool. Click **Start**, point to **Programs**, point to **Administrative Tools**, and then click **Active Directory Sites and Services**. Open this tool and then expand the path **Sites | Default-First-Site-Name | Servers | YourServerName**.

Figure 9-7 The view of AD Sites and Services with NTDS Settings

2. Click **NTDS Settings** and then right-click the connection object between your server and your partner's server. On the menu that appears next, click the **Replicate Now** option and then press **F5** to refresh the display. Make sure that both your computer and your partner's computer are visible in this view. If you do not see your partner's computer, repeat steps 1 and 2 again. For handling additional problems, consult your instructor. If you and your partner are satisfied that replication has occurred, close AD Sites and Services.

3. Now use the Backup utility to perform a backup of the System State data on Server2. Click **Start**, point to **Programs**, point to **Accessories**, click **System Tools**, and then click **Backup**. Click the **Backup** tab and select only the System State box at the bottom of the screen. Start the backup after saving the backup file to **C:\Windows2000.bkf**. The backup tool running should look like Figure 9-8.

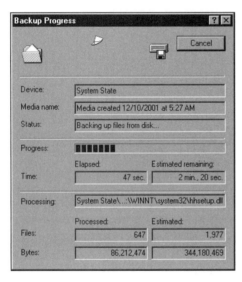

Figure 9-8   The process of backing up System State data

4. After this backup is complete, you can proceed to the rest of the lab.

5. There are several administrative tasks that you need to complete before proceeding to the main part of this lab. You will need to determine the Invocation ID, which is used to identify the replication version of the current database. You will also need to determine the version number of the name attribute for the Users OU.

6. In order to allow the collection of this data, you must first install Windows 2000 Support Tools. To install these tools, you will need the installation media for Windows 2000. Place the CD into the CD tray and then use Explorer to examine the path: *cd_drive\support\tools*. In the Tools folder, double-click the file named **Setup.exe** to install the support tools and accept the installation defaults.

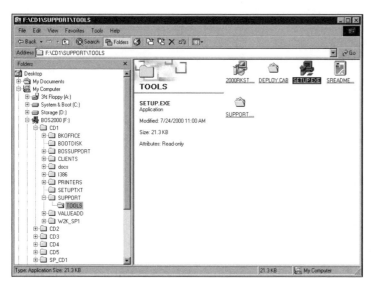

Figure 9-9   The installation path and file name for the Windows 2000 Support Tools

7. After this tool set has been installed, you will be able to continue with the lab.

8. To retrieve the Invocation ID, open a Command Prompt and type the command **repadmin /showreps** *Server1*. Record the Invocation ID in the box below for later use.

Invocation ID #	

9. At the same time, also from the Command Prompt, issue the command **repadmin /showmeta "ou=users,dc=***child_domain_name*,**dc=***parent_domain_name*,**dc=***top_level_domain_name* and then press **Enter**. This is the version number of the name attribute for the OU performing the restoration. Record it in the box below.

Version Number	

10. It is now time for you to perform the actual AD Restoration.

11. Now that the backup is complete, delete an OU from only one computer in your domain. This will be the test for AD Restore Mode.

A few notes and cautions first:
- Perform the AD Restoration from only one computer if working with a partner.
- Read through the remainder of this lab before proceeding further so you understand all the steps.
- Close all open applications.

12. Having completed all three steps in the Caution note above, you are now ready to continue.

13. Restart your domain controller. When the domain controller restarts, you will see the message "For troubleshooting and advanced startup options for Windows 2000 press F8" appear on the monitor. Press **F8**.

14. On the **Advanced Options** menu, choose the **Directory Services Restore Mode** and press **Enter**.

15. Use your Administrator account and password to log into Windows 2000. In each corner of your monitor, you will see "Safe Mode". This is your indication that you are running in Safe Mode, which is needed to perform the restoration of AD.

16. Using the Backup tool, perform a Restore of the OS using the backup file created in Step 3 above. Click **Start**, point to **Programs**, point to **Accessories**, click **System Tools**, and then click **Backup**. When this Restore is complete, you will be prompted to restart the computer. Whether you select Yes or No depends on the type of AD restoration you are performing.

17. If you are performing a Nonauthoritative restore of AD, then you are finished and you may click **Yes**. This is because the Nonauthoritative restore process consists of Restoring using a Current backup of AD and then allowing normal replication with your domain replication partners to bring your AD database to a current state. The Nonauthoritative restore of AD is used for those instances when a domain controller crashes and the database of the machine needs to be restored to a working state with no further involvement of its domain replication partners.

18. If you are performing the Authoritative restore, the process is slightly different. Complete the restore process through Step 16 above and then click **No** because you have additional steps to complete. The additional steps are given below.

    a. Open a Command Prompt, type the command **ntdsutil**, and press **Enter**.

    b. The ntdsutil tool is command-line driven. Before using it, be sure to review the information about the tool contained in the online Help information in Windows 2000 and also in the Windows 2000 Server Resource Kit.

    c. After you have reviewed the information concerning **ntdsutil** from the resources given above, you are ready to proceed with the rest of the lab.

    d. Next, type **authoritative restore** at the ntdsutil prompt and press **Enter**.

    e. To view a list of tool options, type **?** at the authoritative restore prompt.

    f. After reviewing the list of available options for the tool, which option would you select? If you answered **restore subtree**, you are correct.

g. From the authoritative restore prompt, type the following command, where *ou_name* is the name of the OU to be restored: **restore subtree "ou=***ou_name***,dc=***child_domain_name***,dc=***parent_domain_name***,dc=***root_ domain_name***"** and press **Enter**. Click **Yes** to close the Authoritative Restore Confirmation box.

h. Type **quit** twice, then type **exit** to exit **ntdsutil**. Then restart the computer. Log on normally with the Administrator account and password.

i. Check AD. Is the OU that you deleted in Step 11 above back in AD? If so, then your AD Restoration was successful. If not, then repeat the lab and try to determine where the process failed.

19. You would use the Authoritative Restore of AD when an actual AD data object, such as an OU or a Group or an individual user, has been deleted from AD and replication has occurred between all domain controllers so that the deleted object does not exist on any domain controller. The Authoritative Restore informs other domain controllers in the AD domain that the machine performing the restore has the definitive copy of AD and that all domain controllers should pull their AD replication information from this machine.

20. To confirm the restoration of AD, open a Command Prompt and type the command **repadmin /showreps** *Server1* and press **Enter**. Note whether the Invocation returned now is different than the Invocation ID returned in Step 8 above.

21. To confirm the restoration of AD using a different technique, open a Command Prompt and type the command **repadmin /showmeta "ou=users,dc=***child_domain_name***,dc=***parent_domain_name***,dc=***top_level_do main_name*** and then press **Enter**. Compare the version number returned with the version number from Step 9 above. The version number should now be 100,000 greater than the value recorded in Step 9.

LAB 9.5 ACTIVE DIRECTORY BACKUP

Lab Scenario

You have now performed the two kinds of AD Backup: Nonauthoritative and Authoritative. You understand the process; however, you need some definite guidelines that all Administrators in your organization will follow. You need to clearly define: Who, What, When, Where, and Why.

Who: Who can perform an AD backup and restore?

What: What can be backed up and what can be restored?

When: When are the backups to be performed and when are restores to be performed?

Where: Where are the backups and restores to be performed?

Why: Why are the backups and restores to be performed?

These are important points to consider in your support of AD. Having some kind of Administrative plan in place helps you to maintain the validity of your AD implementation.

Objectives

This is a planning exercise. Your task in the lab will be to work with your design team to answer, resolve, and document all of the concerns raised in the scenario outlined above. You must approach this lab as though this is an actual business environment and the future of your job with the company depends on this implementation, which one day it might. After completing this lab, you will be able to:

➤ Develop a usable and consistent plan for backing up AD.

➤ Develop a usable and consistent plan for restoring AD.

➤ Prepare the necessary documentation to enforce corporation-wide backup and restore standards.

➤ Understand which kind of restore to use in which circumstance.

Materials Required

This lab will require the following:

➤ Access to *Windows 2000 Server Resource Kit, Supplement 1*

➤ Access to a Windows 2000 Server with AD installed

➤ The use of the On-line Help files in Windows 2000 Server

➤ Paper, pen, pencils, or a whiteboard

➤ Role playing

Activity Prerequisites

Lab is to be set up as stated in the Lab Setup Guide.

ACTIVITY

Work with your design team to implement the requirements set forth in the scenario for this lab. Prepare and complete a corporate standards document specifying all components of your corporate AD Backup and Restore policy, including, but not necessarily limited to, Users who can perform AD backups, scheduled AD backups, and methods for performing AD backups. Also examine these same issues for AD restores, both for Authoritative and Nonauthoritative restores.

LAB 9.6 ACTIVE DIRECTORY MAINTENANCE

Lab Scenario

You need to maintain the AD and there are tasks that need to be performed, some more frequently than others. You may need to manually defragment the AD database from time to time, particularly if you have been making a large number of additions or deletions from the database. This lab will go over that process.

Objectives

For this lab, you will perform an Offline Defragmentation of the AD database. This is completed from the Directory Services Restore mode. At the end of this lab, you will be able to:

➤ Perform a manual defragmentation of AD.

➤ Check the integrity check of the new file.

➤ Configure AD to use the new file instead of the original file.

Materials Required

This lab will require the following:

➤ Access to a Windows 2000 Server with AD installed

Activity Prerequisites

Lab is to be set up as stated in the Lab Setup Guide.

9

ACTIVITY

1. Restart your domain controller. When the domain controller restarts, you will see the message "For troubleshooting and advanced startup options for Windows 2000, press F8" appear on the monitor. Press **F8**.

2. On the Advanced Options menu, choose the **Directory Services Restore Mode** and press **Enter**.

3. Use your Administrator account and password to log into Windows 2000. In each corner of your monitor, you will see "Safe Mode." This is your indication that you are running in Safe Mode, which is needed to perform the restoration of AD.

4. Open a command prompt and type **ntdsutil** and then press **Enter**. Next, type **files** and then press **Enter**.

5. You are now in the file maintenance view of the ntdsutil tool. Type **info** and then press **Enter** to display the current AD database size. Record this value in the table below.

AD Database Size	

6. From the file maintenance prompt, issue the command to move the AD database. The command is: **move db to c:**. Then press **Enter** to move the file.

7. Next, from the file maintenance prompt, issue the command **move logs to c:** and then press **Enter** to move the file.

8. From the file maintenance prompt, issue the command **info** and then press **Enter** to update the paths to these files.

9. From the file maintenance prompt, issue the command **compact to c:\winnt\ntds** and then press **Enter** to defragment the database.

10. You will now need to redirect AD to the newly compacted files. These steps are also completed from the ntdsutil tool and a Command Prompt environment.

11. With ntdsutil still open, issue the following commands. From the file maintenance prompt, issue the command **set path db c:\winnt\ntds\ntds.dit** and then press **Enter**.

12. From the file maintenance prompt, issue the command **set path backup c:\winnt\ntds\dsadata.bak** and then press **Enter**.

13. From the file maintenance prompt, issue the command: **set path working dir c:\winnt\ntds** and then press **Enter**.

14. From the file maintenance prompt, issue the command: **set path logs c:\winnt\ntds** and then press **Enter**.

15. From the **file maintenance** prompt, issue the command **info** and then press **Enter** to update the paths to these files.

16. Check for any difference in the size of the database after the defragmentation. You may not see a difference, depending on the number of objects in your AD database prior to completing the lab.

17. To perform the integrity check of the AD database, perform the following steps.

18. From the file maintenance prompt, issue the command **integrity** and then press **Enter** to perform the integrity check. You should see a message indicating that the job finished successfully.

19. From the file maintenance prompt, issue the command **quit** to exit the **file maintenance** environment.

20. From the ntdsutil prompt, issue the command **semantic database analysis** and then press **Enter**.

21. From the semantic checker prompt, issue the command **go** and then press **Enter** to perform the analysis of the database.

22. Examine the data returned by the semantic database analysis tool.

23. From the semantic database analysis prompt, issue the command **quit** and then press **Enter**.

24. From the ntdsutil prompt, issue the command **quit** and then press **Enter** to exit ntdsutil and return to a Command Prompt. Type **exit** to close the command prompt and then restart your computer.

LAB 9.7 MANUAL DATABASE CLEANUP

Lab Scenario

Your company is implementing AD and is concerned about whether AD requires any manual maintenance procedures. You and your design team need to meet to consider the following issues. Should you perform manual maintenance or should you depend on AD to maintain itself? When should manual maintenance be performed?

Objectives

This is a planning lab. Meet with your design team and arrive at a set of procedures to determine what, if any, annual maintenance should be performed on the AD database. The issues are:

➤ Does manual maintenance need to be performed?

➤ When should manual maintenance be performed?

➤ What kind of manual maintenance should be performed?

➤ Who should perform it?

After completing this lab, you will be able to:

➤ Perform safe manual maintenance of the AD database.

➤ Address any inquiries from your manager concerning procedures in place.

➤ Understand AD planning issues.

Materials Required

This lab will require the following:

➤ Access to the *Windows 2000 Server Resource Kit, Supplement 1*

➤ Access to a Windows 2000 Server with AD installed

➤ Use of the On-line Help files in Windows 2000 Server

➤ Paper, pen, pencils, or a whiteboard

Activity Prerequisites

Lab is to be setup as stated in the Lab Setup Guide.

ACTIVITY

Work with your design team to implement the requirements set forth in the scenario for this lab. Prepare and complete a corporate standards document specifying all components of your corporate AD Manual Maintenance policy including, but not necessarily limited to, users who can perform AD manual maintenance tasks.

LAB 9.8 BASIC BACKUP PRINCIPLES AND SECURITY

Lab Scenario

One of your largest competitors has closed its doors permanently. Their head IT admin istrator was a good friend of yours and while talking to him you learned that the reaso for the business failure was the compromise of their AD implementation by a disgruntle employee. The other company had not implemented any kind of plan for the backup AD, nor had they done any security planning. As a result, anyone could access the A database and cause harm, which is what happened. You need to prevent this from hap pening to your company.

Objectives

Your objective for this lab is to meet with your design team and arrive at a corporat implementation of an AD Backup and Security plan to try to eliminate any issues th might cause the permanent destruction of your implementation of AD.

After you complete this lab, you will be able to:

➤ Define a Security Policy for your environment.

➤ Define a Backup Policy for your environment.

➤ Successfully implement both policies to restrict access to your AD implementation

Materials Required

This lab will require the following:

➤ Access to *Windows 2000 Server Resource Kit, Supplement1*

➤ Access to two Windows 2000 Server with AD installed

Activity Prerequisites

Lab is to be set up as stated in the Lab Setup Guide.

ACTIVITY

For this lab, work with your design team and formulate a solution to the objectives item- ized above. Apply your experience, both in the classroom and in the real world, to lock down and protect your AD implementation from attacks or misuse. This may include: dis- gruntled employees, natural disasters, man-made disasters, "Acts of God," and any other eventuality you can think of. Make sure that you create a planning document that covers not only what to do to recover from these events, but also how to prevent them in the first place. Be sure to deal with security issues. Remember that this is a corporate envi- ronment and you need to be thorough. Be prepared to present your solution to the class and answer questions or justify your implementation.

Lab 9.9 The Microsoft Backup Utility

Lab Scenario

In keeping with your overall plan to secure AD, you would like to use a backup tool. You know that Windows 2000 includes a Backup Tool; however, you know little about it, so you decide find out more.

Objectives

The goal of this lab is to learn the basic use of the Microsoft Windows 2000 Backup Tool. After you complete this lab, you will be able to:

➤ Use the Backup Wizard to backup your servers.

➤ Use the Backup Wizard to restore your servers.

➤ Create the Windows 2000 Emergency Repair Disk.

➤ Schedule a Backup for unattended backups.

Materials Required

This lab will require the following:

➤ Access to *Windows 2000 Server Resource Kit, Supplement1*

➤ Access to two Windows 2000 Servers with AD installed

➤ Server1

➤ Server2

➤ One 3.5" blank floppy disk per student

Activity Prerequisites

Lab is to be set up as stated in the Lab Setup Guide.

Activity

1. Click **Start**, point to **Programs**, point to **Accessories**, click **System Tools**, and then click **Backup**.

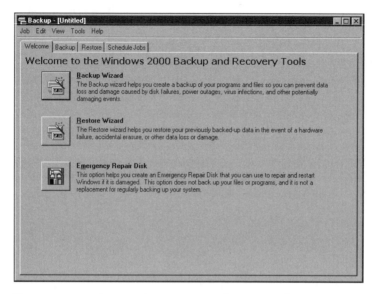

Figure 9-10   The Windows 2000 Backup Wizard Main page showing available options

2. To create a Backup now, click the **Backup Wizard** button and click **Next**. Follow the on-screen instructions and choose what to back up. In this case, choose **Only back up the System State data**, as shown in Figure 9-11, and then click **Next**.

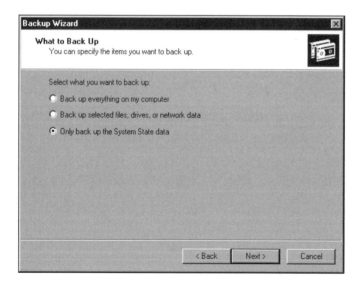

Figure 9-11   The What to Back Up Wizard page and possible selections available

3. Enter the information about where to store the backup file. In this case, accept the default of **C:\Backup.bkf** and then click **Next**.

Be aware that in the real world, this is the least desirable location. For an actual backup procedure, all backup data should be stored either off-line on removable media such as a CDRW, a true backup tape, or an external hard drive/file server. Since you may not have this level of hardware support in your classroom, a local location for this file was chosen.

4. You should now see the screen shown in Figure 9-12.

Figure 9-12   The selected parameters for this Backup session

5. Click **Finish** to start the backup. You will see this screen as the backup process runs (see Figure 9-13).

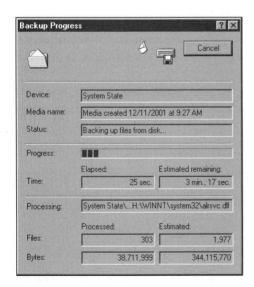

Figure 9-13   An actual backup in progress

6. The information being backed up is the **System State** data, which, as was explained in a previous lab, is all the information on a domain controller (or a user's computer) needed to restore the Domain Controller should it become necessary to do so.

Use the Backup and Restore Wizard to perform a Trial Restoration:

1. Open the Backup program using the same process as was detailed in Step 1 previously.

2. On the Welcome screen (shown previously in Figure 9-10), choose **Restore Wizard**. This will open the screen shown in Figure 9-14.

Figure 9-14   The opening screen of the Restore Wizard

3. Click the **Next** button to display the Restore Wizard/What to Restore selection box. Expand the available media as shown in Figure 9-15 to select an object for restoration after you have selected from the correct media available. In this example, the folder "The Learning Company" has been chosen for a restoration.

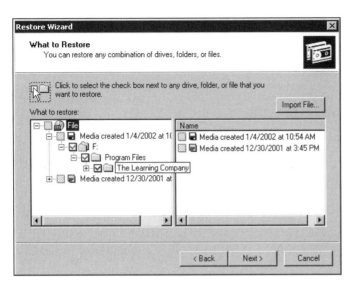

Figure 9-15   Choosing what to restore

4. Click the **Next** button to proceed. On the Completing the Restore Wizard screen, select the **Advanced** button. You have several options available to you when using the Restore Wizard. One of the options is a Trial Restoration, which allows you to restore the backed up files of folders to an alternate location to verify their functionality. Using this option now, click the **Alternate Location** option and then provide a path to the alternate location. When this has been completed, click **Next**. See Figures 9-16 and 9-17.

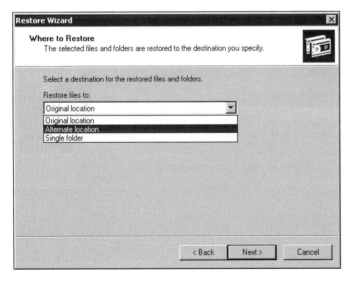

Figure 9-16   Choosing an alternate location for the restored files

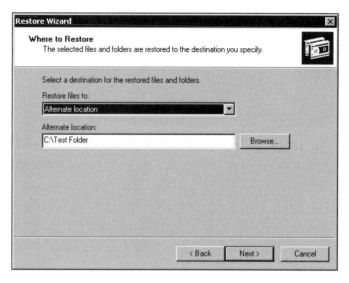

Figure 9-17   Specifying an alternate directory path

5. From the How to Restore screen, accept the default selection of Do not replace the file on my disk (recommended) and click **Next**.

6. On the Advanced Restore Options, be sure to select (if not already selected) the option for Restore security. This option restores NTFS folder and file settings to the state in place when the object was originally backed up and can save you considerable time and work in trying to reset these permissions. Click **Next**.

7. You have now configured the Restore Wizard and you should see a screen similar to the one in Figure 9-18.

Figure 9-18   Completing the Restore Wizard

8. Click **Finish** and on the next dialog, confirm the name of the source file for the restore process. Click **OK** and the restore will begin. If the process was successful, you will see a screen similar to Figure 9-19.

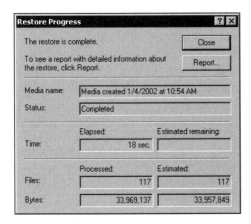

Figure 9-19   The Restore process has been completed

9. You have now completed a restore and may close the Backup Wizard.

Use the Backup Wizard tool to create a Windows 2000 ERD (Emergency Repair Disk):

1. From the **Backup Wizard** tool, choose **Emergency Repair Disk**. You will see the screen shown in Figure 9-20. Be sure to select the option for backing up the registry information.

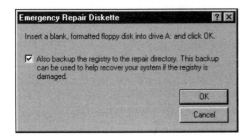

Figure 9-20   The ERD backup registry option

2. Click **OK** to continue. If you have not provided a formatted disk, you will see the message shown in Figure 9-21.

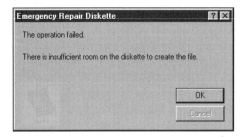

Figure 9-21   You need to use a formatted floppy disk to proceed

3. Click **OK**, format the floppy, and try again. Your **ERD** creation should succeed this time. Place this disk in a safe place. If you need to perform an Emergency Repair to the Registry, you will be prompted for this disk.

 Detailed instructions for using this disk to perform an Emergency Repair can be found in the Windows 2000 Server Resource Kit by searching for **ERD**. Print these instructions out and follow them carefully if you need to perform an Emergency Repair.

 Remember, the ERD is not a bootable floppy. It cannot be used to start the system in the event of a failure.

4. The next procedure is to create a schedule for automated backups of the System State data. To create a new scheduled job, click the **Schedule Jobs** tab in the Backup interface. You will see the screen shown in Figure 9-22.

5. Click the **Add Job** button in the lower portion of the screen. Click **Next** and complete the Wizard. When performing any kind of backup, always select the option to Verify the backup data after the backup is completed. Be sure to supply the appropriate user account, which should have been determined in Lab 9.8. You may need to configure AD to reflect this account.

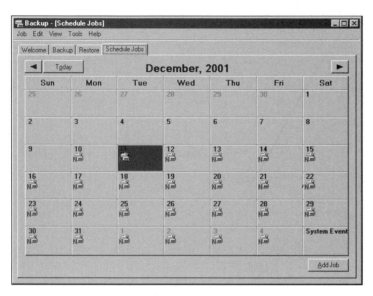

Figure 9-22   The Windows 2000 Backup Wizard Schedule Jobs Wizard calendar view with backups scheduled

9

6. The screen shown in Figure 9–23 is used to set the Backup Job Schedule.

7. Schedule the backup to occur 5 minutes from the current time and click **Next**. The final screen should look similar to one shown in Figure 9–24.

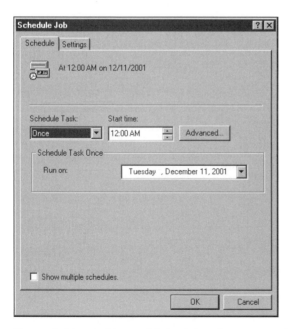

Figure 9-23   Additional Schedule Job settings, days, and times

Figure 9-24   The Backup Wizard confirmation page prior to performing the backup

8. If the backup runs, you were successful. If the backup does not run, redo the lab and try to determine where the problem exists.

IMPLEMENTING GROUP POLICY

Labs included in this chapter

➤ Lab 10.1 Basic Group Policy Concepts

➤ Lab 10.2 Group Policy Objects and Namespace

➤ Lab 10.3 Active Directory Structure and Group Policy

➤ Lab 10.4 Group Policy Inheritance and Processing

➤ Lab 10.5 Group Policy Planning for Active Directory

➤ Lab 10.6 Cross-domain GPO Links and Network Bandwidth

➤ Lab 10.7 Group Policy Implementation

➤ Lab 10.8 Using a GPO Console to Create a GPO

➤ Lab 10.9 Advanced GPO Administration: Filtering, Delegation, Linking

---

Microsoft MCSE Exam #70-217 Objectives	
Objective	Lab
Installing and Configuring Active Directory	10.1, 10.2, 10.3, 10.4, 10.5, 10.6, 10.7, 10.8, 10.9
Configuring, Managing, Monitoring, Optimizing, and Troubleshooting Change and Configuration Management	10.1, 10.2, 10.3, 10.4, 10.5, 10.6, 10.7, 10.8, 10.9
Managing, Monitoring, and Optimizing the Components of Active Directory	10.9
Configuring, Managing, Monitoring, and Troubleshooting Security in a Directory Services Infrastructure	10.4

LAB 10.1 BASIC GROUP POLICY CONCEPTS

Lab Scenario

As the senior IT Administrator for your corporation, you have been given the responsibity of exploring AD Group Policy Objects (GPOs) in preparation for your corporate implmentation of AD and associated GPOs. You need to explore GPOs and what they can for your company. Can you use GPOs to effectively control your users and their compuers? Can you control all of your users or only the ones who work directly on site in officeWhat about your ability to control those users who travel with laptops and the users whwork from home offices? All of these factors need clarification and resolution.

Objectives

The primary goal of this lab is to introduce you to some basic AD GPO conceptAnother purpose is to give you relevant, hands-on experience with one of the most powerful tools for supporting Windows 2000 Active Directory, the *Windows 2000 ServResource Kit, Supplement 1*. This will become an indispensable tool for you in your desigof AD. After completing this lab, you will be able to:

> ➤ Understand some of the uses of AD GPOs.

> ➤ Know what user OSs will support the use of AD GPOs.

> ➤ Know what user OSs will not support the use of AD GPOs.

> ➤ Become familiar with some of the many settings available through the use of GPOs.

> ➤ Become familiar with different sections of the *Windows 2000 Server Resource Kit, Supplement 1.*

> ➤ Use some of the tools available with the Server Resource Kit.

Materials Required

This lab will require the following:

> ➤ Access to *Windows 2000 Server Resource Kit, Supplement 1*

> ➤ Access to a Windows 2000 Server with AD installed

Activity Prerequisites

Lab is to be set up as stated in the Lab Setup Guide.

ACTIVITY

All labs will require the use of the Server Resource Kit and all labs relate to GPO issuesIt may be beneficial to break into teams to work on this lab. Research AD GPOs carefully, using the resources available to you to arrive at answers to the questions below. Theywill serve as a good foundation for the succeeding labs in this chapter.

1. You have users who are working on a secret project for the corporation. They work in the R&D office and their work is of tremendous future value to the company. Refer to the *Windows 2000 Server Resource Kit, Supplement 1* to answer the following questions.

   a. What steps could you take to secure their computers against unauthorized access?

   b. Can you prevent someone from reading files on their computers?

   c. Could you extend this protection to their Pagefile? If so, how?

2. Corporate headquarters has decreed that all corporate desktops shall be identical in appearance and that "...*individual variance will not be tolerated.*" You read this as a mandate to lock down the users' desktops completely to deny access to all user configurable settings.

   a. Is this possible?

   b. If yes, how can it be done?

3. The **BSA** (Business Software Alliance) has been active in your area, checking companies and corporations for unlicensed software. In fact, a company nearby, where your friend works, was just fined $1.5 million for having unlicensed software on their users' computers.

   a. Is there some aspect of AD that you could use to control the software that your users have on their machines?

   b. Is it possible to automatically detect the users' private software and remove it from their systems, while at the same time installing only software covered by your corporate license?

The BSA does exist and they do have legally enforceable rights to pursue software piracy.

4. You are using server-based User Profiles for those users currently running Windows NT 4.0. Every morning when your users begin their business day and all the workstations are turned on, the network suffers a tremendous drop in performance as all of your clients download their network-based profile folders. Since the decision has been made to upgrade all user workstations to Windows 2000, is there some technique in Windows 2000 that will allow a different implementation of this functionality—namely centralized, network-based file storage for your users?

5. Your users like to experiment on their machines at work. As a result, you and your support team spend significant amounts of time each week rebuilding your users' computers. As part of this rebuild process, your rebuild team spends, on average, 1.5 days rebuilding each machine to the user specifications. This amount of time is unacceptable. Ignoring, for the time being, the issue of user experimentation (which is a separate issue), is there a faster rebuild process for the user machines that you can utilize without relying on a disk-imaging

(cloning) process? What you would ultimately like to implement is some kind of unattended installation process.

6. A directive has been issued from corporate to hide all non-essential drives on each user's computer. Additionally, corporate wants the floppy drives and CD-ROMs disabled on machines that are shared by two or more users, but not disabled for all the users on these machines. They should be disabled only for specific users without affecting other users. Is this possible?

LAB 10.2 GROUP POLICY OBJECTS AND NAMESPACE

Lab Scenario

You have decided to begin preliminary design work on your AD GPO implementation. You have assembled your design team, collected materials, and are ready to start work. You company has decided to use a single forest containing a single domain initially. This is subject to change, provided you can justify the change. They have two separate divisions run by different presidents, owned by the same family, sharing the same building, using different names, employing different personnel, and using different web sites with unique Internet names. Each employee is paid by only one company.

The owners of the company wish to support each company separately with separate policies for different divisions in each company. These would support different work units providing totally different services and be billed on separate invoices. They have one shared IT department that supports both companies. One company has a number of employees who not only use Windows 2000 as their OS, but also use non-MS OSs in the course of their work. All machines share the same physical network. The e-mail addresses of both companies are different, yet they share the same e-mail server. They do not currently restrict Internet access for their employees, allowing unlimited connectivity. This must change, owing to a decline in productivity and a recent increase in virus infections.

Objective

The goal of this lab is for you and your design team to complete a preliminary design (subject to later revision) of this company's implementation of AD GPOs at the top level. At this time, you will not make detailed plans on a department-by-department basis. Instead, you will make plans for the implementation on a company-by-company basis, keeping in mind the constraints given in the scenario above. After completing this lab, you will be able to:

➤ Formulate a preliminary design of an AD GPO implementation.

➤ Begin the process of creating individual GPOs based on job function/other constraints.

➤ Implement DNS and Internet connectivity.

➤ Provide some security control.

➤ Understand GPO inheritance.

Materials Required

This lab will require the following:

➤ Access to *Windows 2000 Server Resource Kit, Supplement 1*

➤ Access to a Windows 2000 Server with AD installed

➤ Paper, pen, pencils, whiteboard, and markers

Activity Prerequisites

Lab is to be set up as stated in the Lab Setup Guide. The previous lab in this chapter must be completed.

ACTIVITY

You may assume that this company uses an ISP for DNS services; however, the web sites for each company are maintained in that company on their own MS IIS 4.0 servers. Additionally, they have a single MS Exchange 5.5 server in-house, configured to support two separate e-mail domains, one for each company. The retail package of MS Exchange 2000 is sitting on the owner's desk awaiting installation. The owners of the company have already committed to spending up to, but not more than, $200,000 for upgraded hardware (new servers and infrastructure) and new/upgraded software (workstation/server and applications), provided you and your team can justify the expense. At this point you have the complete, unrestricted backing of the owners of the enterprise.

This is a planning exercise. Gather your design team, assign roles, and complete a plan. There is no one right or wrong answer. Some designs will afford better security than other plans. Some plans will be more flexible than other plans. Each plan will be different. All plans are subject to later revision. These are the basic plans you will implement, with modifications, throughout the remainder of this lab. Design carefully. After each team has completed their design, compare notes and designs in class to view the different implementations. Do not be afraid to incorporate other teams' design elements into your design if you see an advantage in their solution.

10

LAB 10.3 ACTIVE DIRECTORY STRUCTURE AND GROUP POLICY

Lab Scenario

You will now expand on the design work performed in Lab 10.2. Here are some additional details to round out your design:

➤ This is a family-owned business with active, daily participation of the family members.

➤ There are two separate companies, Thisbin Co. and Kronk Designs.

➤ They share: one building, two staffs, two web sites, one IIS server, two e-mail addresses but one e-mail server, one network infrastructure (cabling and Internet connectivity), one receptionist/switchboard operator, and one IT department.

➤ Thisbin Co. is a graphics design house supporting large corporate customers with very tight production schedules. They use a mixture of:

- Windows 2000

- NT 4.0

- Windows 98

- Windows 95

- Apple McIntosh OS 9.

➤ There is no security in place on any machine, including servers, beyond antivirus software, a partially configured third-party hardware-based firewall product, and NT 4.0 Domain accounts for users. Both companies share the same NT 4.0 domain structure for ease of administration.

- The antivirus software is configured to run automatically on servers (one file/print, one Exchange, one IIS 4.0, one NT 4.0 PDC, and two BDCs).

- The antivirus software is not configured to run automatically on the user machines. Some users run an antivirus check as frequently as once every week; others are unaware of what a computer virus is, but are proficient web surfers.

- The McIntosh computers do not have any antivirus software.

- Additionally, you have learned that some individuals have a second computer at home, either a desktop or traveling laptop that is used for doing work. These machines are also the family computer. The machines are used to download files at home and then upload files to floppy disks, which are then transferred to the user's office machines in the morning. The security/antivirus status of these machines is unknown.

➤ Kronk Designs is a design firm that specializes in producing large format advertising media (billboards, designs on cars and trucks, etc.).

➤ They are a smaller company than Thisbin Co., having approximately 20 employees, while Thisbin Co. employs approximately 60 people.

➤ Kronk Designs uses only Windows 2000 with two NT 4.0 servers running as member servers and two Windows 95 workstations that will be replaced within the month. This is a scheduled replacement and does not need to be included in any projected hardware costs. The two NT 4.0 servers run specialized software that is not currently supported on Windows 2000.

➤ Kronk Designs also has antivirus software in place on the user machines, but, like their sister company, it is rarely, if ever, used by the employees.

➤ Kronk Designs employees have unrestricted Internet access using a leased T1 line. This is the same line used by Thisbin Co., whose employees also enjoy completely unrestricted Internet access using a T1 line.

➤ Kronk Designs has fewer mobile/remote users than Thisbin Co. However, the remote users they do have are higher up in the management structure than the majority of Thisbin Co. remote/mobile users.

Objectives

The objective of this lab is to enhance the design created in Lab 10.2. You will use the newly discovered material from this lab and the design you created in Lab 10.2 to redesign/modify your AD GPO planning document. This is exclusively a planning lab. After completing this lab, you will be able to:

➤ Refine an AD GPO design and modify it by incorporating newly discovered features.

➤ Design a flexible implementation of AD GPOs, rather than one that is inflexible and therefore difficult to modify or grow.

➤ Work effectively with outside design teams in designing AD GPOs.

➤ Appreciate that AD and GPO designs are not driven by the needs of the IT department/support staff, but rather by the business needs/concerns of the business or corporation.

10

Materials Required

This lab will require the following:

➤ Access to *Windows 2000 Server Resource Kit, Supplement 1*

➤ Access to a Windows 2000 Server with AD installed

➤ Paper, pen, pencils, whiteboard, and markers

Activity Prerequisites

Lab is to be set up as stated in the Lab Setup Guide. Lab 10-2 must be completed.

ACTIVITY

This is a planning exercise. Assemble your design team, assign roles, and complete a plan. Provide for full, complete integration with the design from Lab 10.2. You will be building on that design and correcting/modifying as you proceed with this design. Design carefully. After each team has completed their design, compare notes and designs in class to view the different implementations.

LAB 10.4 GROUP POLICY INHERITANCE AND PROCESSING

Lab Scenario

As your design for Thisbin Co. and Kronk Designs continues to grow, you realize that the ability to nest certain OUs within other OUs would be an advantage, allowing you to apply a more granular level of GPO control. One of the most important aspects of GPO is their ability to inherit settings from their parent GPOs. You also have the ability to block the inheritance of GPOs from the parent object to the child object. However blocking inheritance is not a management technique. It can needlessly complicate your AD implementation and produce issues with the day-to-day functionality of AD GPO. You are getting closer to your final design of AD GPOs for your clients, Thisbin Co. and Kronk Designs. You need to begin the process of designing for inheritance of their respective GPOs.

Objectives

The goal of this lab is to design your inheritance plan using Figures 10-1 and 10-2, as well as your design documents from the previous labs. After completing this lab, you will be able to:

➤ Design AD to support multiple GPOs and nested GPOs.

➤ Design AD GPOs for efficient application and processing.

➤ Design AD GPOs for inheritance.

➤ Correct previously existing GPO placements and modify current designs.

➤ Work effectively as a design team.

➤ Support a business environment through effective GPO placement and processing.

Materials Required

This lab will require the following:

➤ Access to *Windows 2000 Server Resource Kit, Supplement 1*

➤ Access to a Windows 2000 Server with AD installed

➤ Paper, pen, pencils, whiteboard, and markers

Activity Prerequisites

Lab is to be set up as stated in the Lab Setup Guide. Previous labs in this chapter must be completed.

ACTIVITY

This is a planning exercise. Consult with the rest of your team, and complete a plan. Provide for full, complete integration with the design from Lab 10.3. You will be building on that design and correcting/modifying as you proceed with this design. The design below may be good, or it may have issues. You and your team will make that determination.

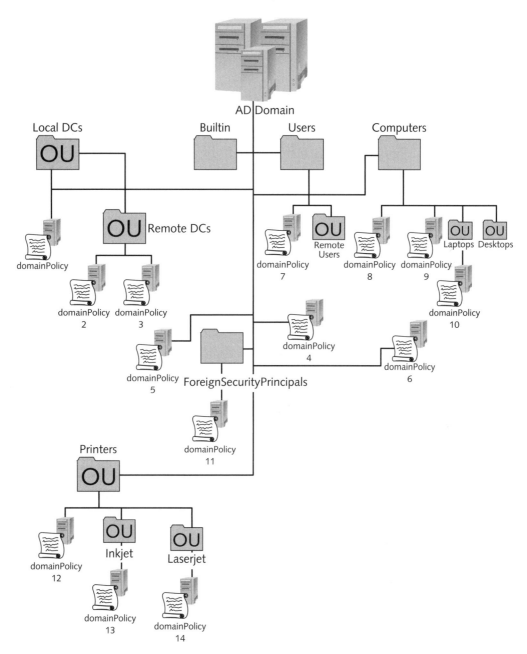

Figure 10-1   An AD design with OUs and GPOs in place

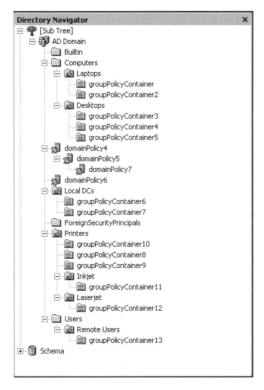

Figure 10-2   A different view of AD with GPOs being applied to the tree

The group policy objects have not been defined. They have been placed on OUs to pro‑
vide an example of placement options and possibilities. Use them along with the constrain‑
from the previous labs to implement your inheritance design.

There is no single right or wrong answer. Some designs will afford better security tha‑
other plans. Each plan will be different. All plans are subject to later revision. These plan‑
will be used to implement, with modifications, your team's AD GPO design throughou‑
the remainder of this lab. After each team has completed their design, compare notes an‑
designs in class to view the different implementations. Do not be afraid to incorporat‑
other teams' design elements into your design if you see an advantage in their solution.

LAB 10.5 GROUP POLICY PLANNING FOR ACTIVE DIRECTORY

Lab Scenario

You have reached the point where you can begin your final design for supporting Thisbir‑
Co. and Kronk Designs with an effectively planned, well-thought-out AD GPO imple‑
mentation. This is the final design-planning event before the actual implementation begins

Objectives

The goal of the lab is to evaluate your AD GPO designs and look for things that can break. This lab is designed as a simulation of the real world. After completing this lab, you will be able to:

➤ Critique your AD GPO designs.

➤ Critique other AD GPO designs.

➤ Understand schematic views of AD with GPO objects in place.

➤ Understand how to apply the concepts of previous labs.

Materials Required

This lab will require the following:

➤ Access to *Windows 2000 Server Resource Kit, Supplement 1*

➤ Access to a Windows 2000 Server with AD installed

➤ Paper, pen, pencils, whiteboard, and markers

Activity Prerequisites

10

Lab is to be set up as stated in the Lab Setup Guide. Previous labs in this chapter must be completed.

ACTIVITY

This is a planning exercise. As you and your design team complete a plan, provide for full, complete integration with the designs from all previous labs. Critique your designs extensively. See if you can introduce problems into your design before you actually sit down at the computer keyboard. Look at the designs of other teams. Perform the same tasks. Critique their designs. Look for things that can break in their designs. Look for the unexpected. Be sure to make any comments constructive and be prepared to justify your design decisions to other teams.

LAB 10.6 CROSS-DOMAIN GPO LINKS AND NETWORK BANDWIDTH

Lab Scenario

From your review of Lab 10.5, you may have found GPOs in Thisbin Co. that would work very well in Kronk Designs and GPOs in Kronk Designs that are exactly what you wanted for Thisbin Co. If this is the case, you may now implement an additional feature of AD GPOs—the ability to link GPOs from one domain to another. It is not necessary to create duplicate GPOs in two separate domains. You can logically link GPOs to domains or OUs to provide functionality and assure that only one copy of the desired GPO is actually in place at any time. This serves the additional benefit of making certain

that any changes to this GPO are changed in only one location, not several different one
There is a price to pay for functionality, however, and the price is additional networ
bandwidth use caused by the links. In addition, if the parent object of the linked GPO
unavailable, then your linked GPO will be unavailable as well. Can you accommodate th
in your environment?

Objectives

The goal of this lab is to analyze the AD GPO designs produced by your design team fc
Thisbin Co. and Kronk Designs and identify possible linkage. After completing this lal
you will be able to:

➤ Identify GPOs that could be linked to produce a more efficient implementation of AD.

➤ Identify GPOs that should not be linked and must remain within their own AD
structure.

➤ Understand the benefits and risks associated with linking.

➤ Review AD designs looking for possible linkage candidates.

Materials Required

This lab will require the following:

➤ Access to *Windows 2000 Server Resource Kit, Supplement 1*

➤ Access to a Windows 2000 Server with AD installed

➤ Paper, pen, pencils, whiteboard, and markers

Activity Prerequisites

Lab is to be set up as stated in the Lab Setup Guide. Previous labs in this chapter must be
completed.

ACTIVITY

Assemble your design team again to review your AD GPO design. Is there any duplica-
tion of effort in the design? If so, could it be removed or reduced by implementing linked
GPOs? Do you have the available bandwidth to support the linking of the GPOs? Will
the linkage introduce any security holes into your AD design that did not exist before?
Remember that by conservative estimates, 75% of all hacking occurring in a corporate
environment originates not from external sources, but from internal sources (employees).
Does your linkage of GPOs increase this risk? Be prepared to defend your choices.
Examine the designs of the other teams to review their designs as well.

LAB 10.7 GROUP POLICY IMPLEMENTATION

Lab Scenario

You have now completed approximately 90% of GPO planning. It is time to implement your design. Your presentation to the owners has been scheduled for tomorrow morning. You need to prepare for the presentation.

Objectives

Your goal for this lab is to prepare a professional presentation for the corporation that conveys the reasons for implementing your design. After completing this lab, you will be able to:

➤ Evaluate the complexity of your GPO plan.

➤ Prepare final documentation for your AD GPO design.

➤ Deliver an effective presentation about your AD GPO implementation plan.

Materials Required

This lab will require the following:

➤ Access to *Windows 2000 Server Resource Kit, Supplement 1*

➤ Access to a Windows 2000 Server with AD installed

➤ Paper, pen, pencils, whiteboard, and markers

Activity Prerequisites

Previous labs in this chapter must be completed.

ACTIVITY

Prepare your final documentation for your AD GPO designs. You will be presenting them in front of the class at the conclusion of this lab. Be prepared to justify all aspects of your design. If you can prepare a rough estimate of any monies to be spent to implement your design, do so. Remember that you are not simply presenting to your classmates. You are presenting to the owners of the company. The rest of the class needs to assume the role of owners while you are presenting your design. Ask critical questions. Try to think of any issues you may have missed. Did you design something that is so complicated that it cannot be easily administered? Will it serve the original design goal that was first set out?

10

LAB 10.8 USING A GPO CONSOLE TO CREATE A GPO

Lab Scenario

The owners of the company have accepted your AD GPO design. It is now time implement it in AD. You will use the GPO Console in AD to configure your GPOs functionality.

Objectives

The goal of this lab is to use Active Directory Users and Computers to implement yo GPOs into AD. After completing this lab, you will be able to:

➤ Implement your GPOs into AD using Active Directory Users and Computers.

➤ Create OUs and GPOs in a variety of different organizational structures.

➤ Use the various settings in the GPO Console to complete your tasks.

Materials Required

This lab will require the following:

➤ Access to *Windows 2000 Server Resource Kit, Supplement 1*

➤ Access to a Windows 2000 Server with AD installed

Activity Prerequisites

Lab is to be set up as stated in the Lab Setup Guide. Previous labs in this chapter must b completed.

ACTIVITY

You will use Active Directory Users and Computers to implement your GPOs into AI However, since the AD implementation of the classroom probably does not match tha of your design labs, you will not be completing a full implementation. Instead, familiar ize yourself with the use of the MMC GPO Console tool. Understand that in the cur rent implementation of AD there are over 400 separate GPOs that can be applied again: the computer, against the user, or against both. You should have resolved all conflicts wit your GPOs by this point. Also, be aware of the fact that if you use Microsoft Visi Enterprise Edition, it is possible to design your AD and GPO implementation using tha tool. Then you can import directly into AD without having to manually create objects a the GUI interface. The process of creating OUs and GPOs can also be scripted an applied against AD using that process as well. Experiment with the GPO Console an explore the different settings.

AB 10.9 ADVANCED GPO ADMINISTRATION: FILTERING, DELEGATION, LINKING

Lab Scenario

Your AD GPOs have been in place for a week now and you are discovering some issues with them. Some OUs are receiving GPOs that were not intended for them; users who should be able to complete tasks cannot because they are being controlled by GPOs that should not be applied to them. Other users are making business cases for individual variances of GPOs. In addition, the issue of controlling the GPOs has arisen, along with the need to revisit the linking of GPOs across the network. You and your design team need to fine-tune the process in order to achieve the desired results.

Objectives

The goal of this lab is to identify newly discovered issues with your AD GPO implementation and create a procedures manual.

Materials Required

This lab will require the following:

➤ Access to *Windows 2000 Server Resource Kit, Supplement 1*

➤ Access to a Windows 2000 Server with AD installed

Activity Prerequisites

Lab is to be set up as stated in the Lab Setup Guide. Previous labs in this chapter must be completed.

ACTIVITY

In order to resolve these issues, you and your design team need to create a procedures manual listing what can and what cannot be done to and with AD GPOs. Also, you need to identify who is authorized to perform those tasks. You will also need to address the issues of individual variances in GPO application. What is the proper level of justification for such variances, and which officer of the company is going to approve the individual variances, if any? You need to use your planning documents and revisit your linked GPOs as well. Apparently some issues have arisen with these. Since a LAN environment interconnects your employer, Thisbin Co./Kronk Designs, the issues you are experiencing with linked GPOs are probably minimal in terms of bandwidth usage. However, what would happen if each company had remote offices that were connected by demand dial routing? What kind of issues would your infrastructure and users experience then? Is there any documentation that details this functionality in AD for the GPOs? Try consulting the *Windows 2000 Server Resource Kit, Supplement 1*.

10

A more difficult issue to control is that of delegation of authority over the GPOs. Who
going to be the responsible party for the GPOs you implemented? Some individuals wh
want to receive delegated permissions to GPOs for their OUs have already approached yo
Additionally, are there some individuals in the company now who do not have delegate
rights to GPOs, but probably should? Is there a central Human Resources authority
place? Is it logical to assign them the delegated permission to create new users as ne
employees are hired? Is it also logical to assign delegated permission to the users to allo
them to change only their own personal information, such as home telephone numbe
street, and address, etc.? Consider these issues using the resources available to you. Th
Windows 2000 Server Resource Kit, Supplement1 contains most of this information. Do no
be afraid to redesign your AD GPO implementation slightly to resolve these issues. AD wa
intended to be modified to meet changing needs.

MANAGING USER ENVIRONMENTS WITH GROUP POLICY

Labs included in this chapter

➤ Lab 11.1 Basic Scripting

➤ Lab 11.2 Windows Scripting Host

➤ Lab 11.3 Start Up, Shut Down, Log On, and Log Off Scripts

➤ Lab 11.4 Assigning Scripts Through Group Policy

➤ Lab 11.5 Controlling the User Environment

➤ Lab 11.6 Administrative Templates for Computers and Users

➤ Lab 11.7 Supporting and Implementing User Profiles for Down-level Clients

➤ Lab 11.8 Supporting and Implementing Folder Redirection for Windows 2000 Clients

➤ Lab 11.9 Comparing and Contrasting User Profiles and Folder Redirection

Microsoft MCSE Exam #70-217 Objectives	
Objective	Lab
Configuring, Managing, Monitoring, Optimizing, and Troubleshooting Change and Configuration Management	11.1, 11.2, 11.3, 11.4, 11.5, 11.6, 11.7, 11.8, 11.9
Managing, Monitoring, and Optimizing the Components of Active Directory	11.1, 11.2, 11.3, 11.4

LAB 11.1 BASIC SCRIPTING

Lab Scenario

In your day-to-day duties at Lonestar Graphics, you are called upon to complete many repetitive tasks, such as creating new user accounts, creating new folders, configuring shared folder permissions, and others. These manual operations are consuming a great deal of your daily time in the office and are preventing you from completing other more vital tasks. In addition, while you are overworked with these manual tasks, your assistants are underutilized because they lack the administrative skill set to complete these tasks. You need to investigate other options to facilitate your daily workload. You decide to investigate scripting as a possible solution to your administrative overload.

Objectives

The goal of this lab is to learn some simple scripting techniques that require only Command Prompt environment or Windows Notepad for creation of scripts. After completing this lab, you will be able to:

➤ Write simple administrative scripts.

➤ Debug simple scripts.

➤ Understand the difference between the *.bat and *.cmd extensions.

Materials Required

This lab will require the following:

➤ Access to a Windows 2000 Server named *Server1*

➤ Access to *Windows 2000 Server Resource Kit, Supplement 1*

Activity Prerequisites

Lab is to be set up as stated in the Lab Setup Guide.

ACTIVITY

1. From *Server1*, log on to your domain with a domain administrator account.

2. Click **Start**, click **Run**, and then type **notepad** and click **OK**.

3. In the Notepad window, type the following command: **echo Hello, world!** Be sure to press **Enter** one time at the end of the string. See Figure 11-1.

4. Click **File** on the menu bar, and then click **Save As**.

5. In the Save As dialog box, be sure that the Save in drop-down list points to **My Documents**. In the File Name dialog box, type the file name as **Hello.bat**, set the Save as Type to **All Files** and set Encoding to **ANSI**. See Figure 11-2.

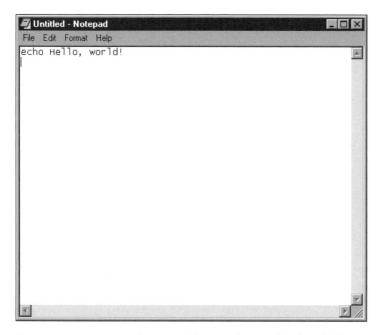

Figure 11-1 Notepad view of the "Hello, world" batch file

Figure 11-2 Using the Save As dialog box to save "Hello, world"

6. Once the settings have been configured, click **Save**. Then close **Notepad.**

7. Click **Start**, click **Run**, and then type **cmd** to open a Command Prompt.

8. At the C:\Documents and Settings\Administrator prompt, type
   cd\documents and settings\administrator\my documents.

9. Type **dir** to list the contents of this directory. You should see the file **Hello.bat**. If you don't see this file, perform a search for it and move the file to the path given in Step 8 above.

10. Return to the Command Prompt and type **cls** to clear this screen. Once the screen is cleared, type **hello** and examine the results. At the command prompt type this text: **rename hello.bat hello.cmd.**

11. At the command prompt, type **hello** again and see the results.

ACTIVITY

Windows 2000 supports two different extensions for batch files, .bat and .cmd. The extension .bat is from the MS-DOS world, while the extension .cmd is from IBM OS/2. Either will function in a Windows 2000 environment and they can be used interchangeably. Now you can refine and enhance your scripting with another short exercise.

1. With the Command Prompt still open, type **edit**. The MS-DOS Editor for Windows 2000 opens, as shown in Figure 11-3. As you explore this tool, you will discover that your mouse does not function here. You will need to use the keyboard and function keys in this interface. However, the MS-DOS Editor will produce the most consistent results for the creation of batch files and scripts.

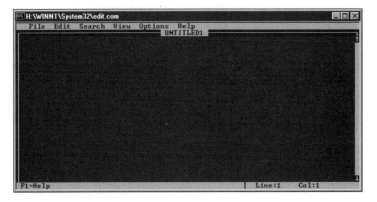

Figure 11-3   A view of the Edit tool

2. With the Edit tool open on your Desktop, type the following lines of text, being careful to press **Enter** at the end of each line.

The line that begins with *copy "c:* must be typed on one line.

```
mkdir c:\temp1
cd c:\temp1
mkdir temp_files
copy "c:\documents and settings\administrator\
my documents\hello.cmd" "c:\temp1\temp_files\*.*"
call c:\temp1\temp_files\hello
del c:\temp1\temp_files\*.* /q
dir c:\temp1\temp_files
```

3. After typing these lines, press **Enter** a final time. See Figure 11-4.

Figure 11-4   A view of the program listing in Edit

4. Press **Alt+F.** Then, in the File menu, use your cursor keys to select **Save As.** For the File name in the Save As dialog box, type this path:

```
c:\documents and settings\administrator\my documents\
complex.bat
```

5. Press **Enter** to save the file. See Figure 11-5.

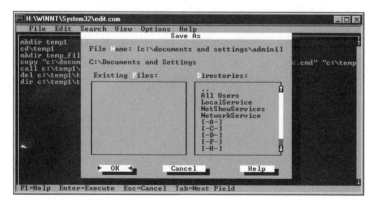

Figure 11-5   The Save As dialog box in Edit

6. Open a new Command Prompt and type **complex** at the command prompt. Then press **Enter**.

7. Now analyze what this batch file did. What are the results of your analysis?

This is a small lab to introduce you to some of the functionality of scripting. As you have just seen, almost any command that can be entered at the Command Prompt can be made part of a batch file or script. This functionality will be appreciated more when you have a chance to examine some of the command line tools included with the Windows 2000 Server Resource Kit. You will now proceed to more advanced topics.

LAB 11.2 WINDOWS SCRIPTING HOST

Objectives

The goal of this lab is to provide a brief introduction to the Windows Scripting Host which is a script execution environment that allows both VB script and J script to run in a Windows environment using Start Up, Shut Down, Log On, and Log Off scripts. This lab will briefly introduce you to the Windows Scripting Host in both the GUI interface mode and the command line interface mode. You are encouraged to read additional material on the Windows Scripting Host to develop additional skills using this powerful tool. After completing this lab, you will be able to:

➤ Write simple scripts to run in a GUI environment.

➤ Write simple scripts to run in a command line environment.

➤ Understand the difference between the two modes.

Materials Required

This lab will require the following:

➤ Access to a computer running Windows 2000 Server

➤ Access to the *Windows 2000 Server Resource Kit, Supplement 1*

Activity Prerequisites

Lab is to be set up as stated in the Lab Setup Guide.

ACTIVITY

1. Click **Start**, click **Run**, and type **notepad**.

2. When Notepad opens, type the following line of text and press Enter at the end of the line. See Figure 11-6.
   Wscript.Echo "Hello, world"

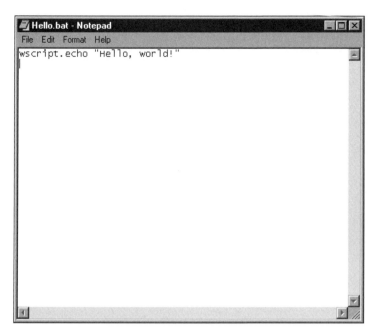

Figure 11-6   Notepad view of the "Wscript Hello, world" vbs script

11

3. In Notepad, click **File**, click **Save As**, and, in the File Name box, type **c:\hello.vbs**

4. Close Notepad.

5. To run your script in a GUI environment, click **Start**, click **Run**, and, in the Run box, type **wscript.exe c:\hello.vbs**. Click **OK**. See Figures 11-7 and 11-8.

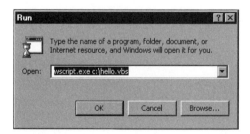

Figure 11-7   How to run "Hello.vbs"

Figure 11-8   The result of running "Hello.vbs" from Wscript

6. When you have finished, click **OK**. Then open a Command Prompt by clicking **Start**, clicking **Run**, and then typing **cmd**. At the prompt, type **cscript.exe c:\hello.vbs**

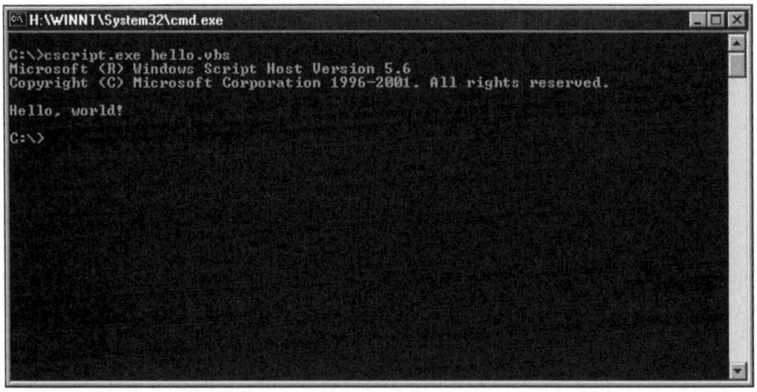

Figure 11-9   The result of running "Hello.vbs" from Cscript

7. When you have finished, type **exit** to close the Command Prompt window.

8. To examine a list of options that are available with the Windows Scripting Host GUI version, click **Start**, click **Run**, and type **wscript //?** in the Run line. Click **OK** and examine the Windows Script Host dialog box that opens next. You may also right-click the file **Hello.vbs**, select **Properties**, and then click the **Script** tab.

9. For the command line version of Windows Script Host, from the Command Prompt type **cscript.exe //?** to examine these optional switches.

10. When you are finished, close the Command Prompt and log off.

Lab 11.3 Start Up, Shut Down, Log On, and Log Off Scripts

Lab Scenario

You need to automate the start-up process for your users and their machines. Your users need to map to network drives at system start. In addition, certain programs need to run to provide full functionality for the users. Some of these scripts need to run at system start no matter which user logs on to the computer, and others are user-specific. You would also like to be able to reverse this process; that is, you would like scripts to run that could un-map network drives at log off and run certain programs at power off for the users. You need to implement the appropriate kind of scripts.

Objectives

The goal of this lab is to create some basic scripts for inclusion in a later lab. This is a paper-based planning exercise that does not require the use of a computer. You and your partner/team will work together to formulate a series of effective and efficient scripts for controlling not only users, but also the user computers. Several different job categories exist within the company, along with several different operating systems. Your job will be to bring order to mayhem. After completing this lab, you will be able to design different types of scripts based on an analysis of:

➤ Users and their needs for job productivity

➤ Computers and their different operating systems

➤ The company and its desire/goals to reduce the Total Cost of Ownership (TCO)

➤ The potential conflicts arising from the first three items listed here

Activity Prerequisites

➤ Some prior computer experience

➤ A lab partner or team

➤ Paper and pencils

➤ Access to *Windows 2000 Server Resource Kit, Supplement 1*

ACTIVITY

11

The table below contains information gathered during your preliminary interviews with company employees and executives. You will also find information concerning the different operating systems in your environment. The corporation has decided not to implement Active Directory Group Policy Objects at this time. Therefore, the scripts that you create will need to be delivered/assigned in the conventional manner, using conventional scripting techniques. Remember to look for conflicting script options when doing your planning, such as someone being joined to a shared resource that they should not have access to. Does someone need access to a NetWare or Unix server at logon?

You are not to actually create scripts. Instead, you are to complete all aspects of the script creation process up to the point of actually coding scripts.

Table 11-1

Operating Systems	Mapped Drives	Shared Machines	Programs
Windows 2000	M: *Unix* T: *MS* X:*NDS*	Yes	Backup; Antivirus
Windows NT 4.0	M: *Unix* X: *MS*	Yes	Backup; Antivirus
Windows ME	X: *NDS*	No	Antivirus
Windows 98	M: *MS*	No	Antivirus
Windows 95	M: *MS*	No	Antivirus

LAB 11.4 ASSIGNING SCRIPTS THROUGH GROUP POLICY

Lab Scenario

You have created basic scripts, you have an understanding of the Windows Scripting Host, and you have some basic designs for several different administrative scripts. Now that startup, shutdown, logon, and logoff scripts have been created, Corporate Headquarters has directed you to implement Active Directory Group Policy Objects for the Windows 2000 users. You will need to plan your Group Policy Object (GPO) implementation carefully before you begin the actual assignment process. You may need to redesign or redistribute both computers and users to design an efficient Active Directory (AD) implementation.

You need to ask yourself the following important questions:

➤ Are you designing for efficient logon for the users or efficient domain replication for you?

➤ Do you have any servers in your environment that require scripts?

➤ Do you have domain controllers that are connected to the Headquarters domain via a WAN connection or are all domain controllers on the same LAN hook up?

You will also need to take into account administration of the scripts once they are assigned through the GPO process. As the Domain Administrator, will you manage the GPO process on a day-to-day basis or would you prefer to delegate authority to other responsible parties within the organization? If you plan to delegate, you may decide to use the Delegation of Control wizard. Where in AD should you implement various scripts/GPOs to maximize the Inheritance Property of the GPO?

Objectives

The goal of this lab is to implement Active Directory Group Policy Objects for the Windows 2000 users. This is a design lab. The implementation details are left to the students and their design partners/design teams. After completing this lab, you will have a preliminary understanding of:

➤ Designing AD for GPO implementation.

➤ Applying scripts to control users.

➤ Applying scripts to control computers.

➤ Designing for replication considerations.

➤ Designing for logon considerations.

➤ Designing for delegation of authority.

Materials Required

This lab will require the following:

➤ Access to a Windows 2000 Server

➤ Access to the *Windows 2000 Server Resource Kit, Supplement 1*

Activity Prerequisites

Lab is to be set up as stated in the Lab Setup Guide.

ACTIVITY

Working as part of a design team, you will now design the implementation of your AD Scripts. To accomplish this:

➤ Determine where the scripts should be assigned, how they should be assigned, and to whom they should be assigned.

➤ Look at such aspects as replication considerations, down-level clients, any issues with time zones, efficient log on for the clients, and delegation of authority (if any) for the maintenance of the scripts.

➤ Ask yourself who the responsible party is for authorizing the creation of these scripts and who has the final say as to which users will or will not be assigned scripts.

11

LAB 11.5 CONTROLLING THE USER ENVIRONMENT

Lab Scenario

You and your administrative team have created several different kinds of scripts for several different kinds of users, both users and computers. However, it is becoming obvious that some of your users are subverting your scripts and reconfiguring their machines, thereby opening up your corporate environment to many different problems. Pernicious virus infections have shown a dramatic increase, particularly among the Windows 2000 users. Management is concerned because, although the employees seem to be spending the same amount of time at work, productivity has decreased recently, along with profits. Expenses, on the other hand, have increased markedly. The ISP monthly bill has almost doubled and there have been issues with miscellaneous supplies, such as print cartridges and toner for the color laser printer, being used up faster than historical trends from last year would indicate. Additionally, inappropriate mailings have been arriving at Corporate Headquarters addressed to non–existent employees. Several key production servers, which formerly ran efficiently, are now experiencing difficulties. Your key production server, which runs Microsoft Windows NT 4.0 Server as a member server, has been experiencing problems with virus infections, even though it does not have an Internet connection.

Obviously, something needs to be done quickly. The Executive wants action from you and your design team right away. As part of your corrective action, you have received the backing of the CEO to implement stringent GPOs for all Windows 2000 users and their computers. Your job and the job of your design team will be to design and implement these GPOs. You will need to consider all aspects of GPO design for both security and efficiency. You may alter your current AD design as needed, but be prepared to justify each modification. You may also specify additional hardware and/or operating systems (up to $150,000) if these expenditures can be justified in terms of securing the corporate environment. You may not redesign the network infrastructure or segment the network. Owing to corporate politics, you may not implement a proxy server or firewall.

Objectives

The goal of this lab is to design and implement GPOs. After completing this lab, you will be able to:

➤ Design AD GPOs for securing the users at their workstations.

➤ Design AD GPOs for securing the workstations.

➤ Restrict access to web sites per corporate guidelines.

➤ Control the software installation procedures.

➤ Configure the desktop.

➤ Restrict remote users and laptop users.

➤ Secure domain controllers and other servers.

Materials Required

This lab will require the following:

➤ Access to two computers running Windows 2000 Server

■ Server1

■ Server2

➤ Access to the *Windows 2000 Server Resource Kit, Supplement 1*

Activity Prerequisites

Lab is to be set up as stated in the Lab Setup Guide.

ACTIVITY

In this lab you will need to work with your design team to create GPOs for your AD environment. Use the objectives listed above as a starting point and arrive at a design. Be certain to involve all members of your design team and draw on their experience and knowledge.

LAB 11.6 ADMINISTRATIVE TEMPLATES FOR COMPUTERS AND USERS

Lab Scenario

As part of your overall design work of locking down your company's users and their computers, you have configured GPOs for the Windows 2000 users and their computers. However, you also have some Microsoft Windows NT 4.0 machines and users in your environment. Some of these down-level machines are workstations and others are servers. Your Windows 2000 users are being controlled by the AD GPOs. You will need to design and implement Administrative Templates for these Windows NT 4.0 machines. Additionally, some of your Windows 2000 users and their computers need settings applied that cannot be implemented through GPOs because these machines, for reasons beyond your control, do not belong to your domain. However, you can implement these settings by using the Administrative Templates feature for Windows 2000. The same process can also be applied to Windows NT 4.0 machines, as well as to Windows 98 and Windows 95, although using a different tool.

Objectives

The goal of this lab is to learn how to create Administrative settings for users and computers and apply them against the Registry of machines to control the users and their computers. After completing this lab, you will be able to:

> Open the System Policy Editor.

> Configure System Policies for the users.

> Configure System Policies for the computers.

> Understand how to create the same kind of policies for down-level operating systems such as:

- Microsoft Windows NT 4.0

- Microsoft Windows 98

- Microsoft Windows 95

Materials Required

This lab will require the following:

> Access to a Windows 2000 Server

> The planning document from Lab 11.5 above

> Access to the *Windows 2000 Server Resource Kit, Supplement 1*

Activity Prerequisites

Lab is to be set up as stated in the Lab Setup Guide.

ACTIVITY

1. Working with your design team, determine what settings, security and otherwise, should be implemented for all users and all machines, regardless of operating system used. Compile this information into a table divided into two sections, one for users and one for computers. At this time, do not differentiate between workstations and servers, or different operating systems.

2. After you have created these tables, complete the following steps to open the System Policy Editor.

The System Policy Editor works by editing the Registry directly. It can produce conditions in the Registry that prevent the computer that is running the tool from starting. Be certain what settings you are applying before closing the tool to accept the changes.

3. Click **Start**, click **Run**, and then type **poledit** and click **OK**. This will open the **System Policy Editor**. The tool interface opens with an empty screen, which is correct, as shown in Figure 11-10.

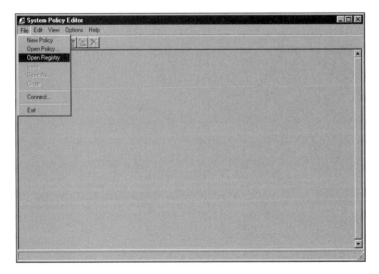

Figure 11-10 Viewing the System Policy Editor File Menu options

4. On the System Policy Editor menu bar, click **File** and then click **Open Registry**. You should now see two icons in the POLEDIT console. The icon on the left is labeled Local Computer and the right icon is labeled Local User, as shown in Figure 11-11.

5. Double-click each icon and examine the contents of the resulting Properties box. You will notice that each Properties box has several expandable trees contained within, which expand into more expandable trees. Open one of these new trees and examine the settings.

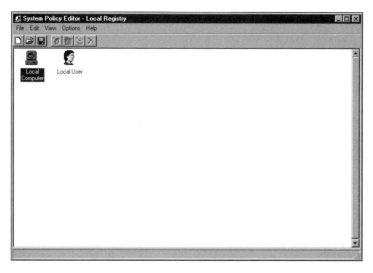

Figure 11-11   The System Policy Editor showing the Local Registry icons for Local
Computer and Local User

6. As an example, expand the path **Local User | Control Panel | Display**.
Under Display, you will see the setting Restrict Display with a check box.
Click **Display** and a list of five different display setting restrictions will appear
in the lower section labeled Settings for Restrict display. See Figure 11-12.

11

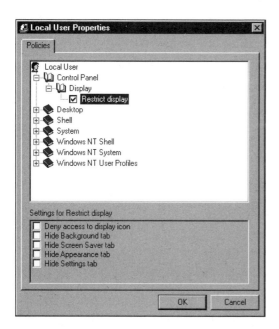

Figure 11-12   Expanded Local User Properties for Control Panel\Display restrictions

7. These settings can be made active by checking the top-level Restrict display option. After this check box is selected, any of the other child settings can be selected.

8. Examine the rest of the settings in both icons to familiarize yourself with them. Your next step will be to create a sample file for your users and machines. Click **Cancel** to close this dialog box and return to the default view for System Policy Editor.

9. Complete the following steps on any domain controller belonging to your classroom domain environment. This is a sample template to illustrate the procedure involved.

    a. With System Policy Editor open, click **File**, and then click **New Policy**.

    b. Then click **Edit** and click **Add Computer**. Add a computer in the classroom environment by typing the name of a computer and then clicking **OK**. See Figures 11-13 and 11-14.

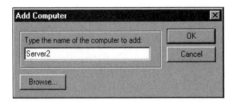

Figure 11-13   The Systems Policy Editor Add Computer dialog box

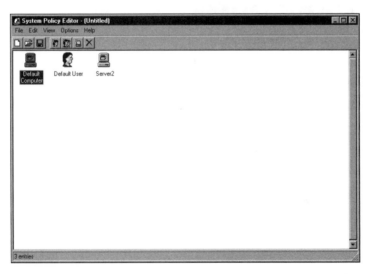

Figure 11-14   System Policy Editor with Server2 added to the Policy view

c. Double-click the new icon named **computer_name** from Step b above.

d. Expand the setting for the **Windows NT System**, and then expand **Logon**.

e. Click the **Logon banner** setting and, in the Caption box, type **Important Notice**.

f. In the Text box, type **Do not attempt to log on unless you are an authorized user.**

g. Also click **Do not display last logged on user name**, and then click **OK** to close the computer_name Properties box.

h. Click **File**, click **Save**, and then save to the path: **C:\SYSVOL\sysvol\<domain name>\SCRIPTS** using the file name **NTCONFIG**. The extension **pol** is added automatically when the file is saved.

 The default path is *system_root:*\winnt\sysvol*domain_name*\scripts. You may have a different path. If you don't find this path, then perform a search for scripts to produce the correct directory path.

10. To test the effects of your new settings, using the machine named in Step c above, log off the network and then log on to the network. Did you see anything different? Repeat this process and you should now see the new settings.

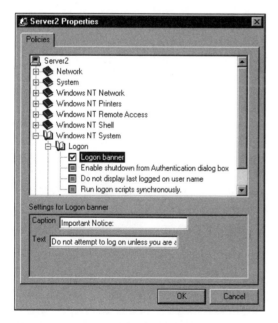

Figure 11-15   Configuring the Server2 Logon Banner and Logon Caption

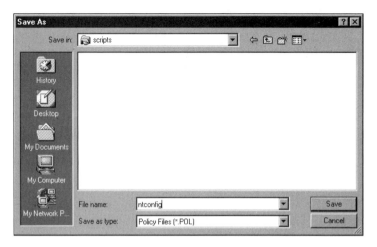

Figure 11-16   The System Policy Editor Files\Save As dialog box with the ntconfig file

These steps will work for Windows 2000 and Windows NT 4.0 machines and users. The process is slightly different for Windows 98 and Windows 95 machines and users. For complete details, refer to the document Prof_Policies.doc on the Microsoft Windows 2000 home page. Now, using this process and the table you completed earlier, configure system policies for your domain users and computers.

LAB 11.7 SUPPORTING AND IMPLEMENTING USER PROFILES FOR DOWN-LEVEL CLIENTS

Lab Scenario

You have locked down your users and their computers, but you need to achieve additional functionality for your environment. Specifically, you would like to centralize the user backups to remove from the users the responsibility of backing up their own work on a daily basis. Corporate Headquarters has also added additional directives, including the directive that all users will have the standard corporate desktop on their computers. Individual variations will not be allowed.

You and your design team will achieve this level of functionality by means of User profiles. User profiles can be implemented for both Windows 2000 and Windows NT 4.0; however, Windows 2000 achieves enhanced functionality by making use of Folder Redirection through GPOs. For the Windows NT 4.0 users, your only way to achieve compliance is User Profiles.

Objectives

The goal of this lab is to show you how to configure User Profiles for down-level clients running Windows 2000 and Windows NT 4.0. After completing this lab, you will be able to:

➤ Design User Profiles for Windows 2000.

➤ Design User Profiles for Windows NT 4.0.

➤ Implement the User Profiles as either roaming profiles or mandatory profiles.

➤ Save and apply the profiles.

➤ Troubleshoot the profiles.

Materials Required

This lab will require the following:

➤ Access to two computers running Windows 2000 Server

  ▪ Server1

  ▪ Server2

➤ Access to the *Windows 2000 Server Resource Kit, Supplement 1*

Activity Prerequisites

Lab is to be set up as stated in the Lab Setup Guide.

ACTIVITY

First you will need to define the appropriate user profile settings for your environment. For the purposes of this exercise, you will use some simple settings consisting of configuring a default desktop for your users that cannot be changed.

1. Create a new user account in AD named **TestProfile**. Assign a password of *profile* to this account. After the account has been created in the domain, log on to the domain using this account from Server2. After logging into the domain, log off of the account and log back on as an administrator on Server2.

2. After logging on, right-click **My Computer**, click **Properties**, and then click the **User Profiles** tab. Verify that the domain user account TestProfile actually did log on to Server2. After verifying this information, log off Server2. See Figure 11-17.

11

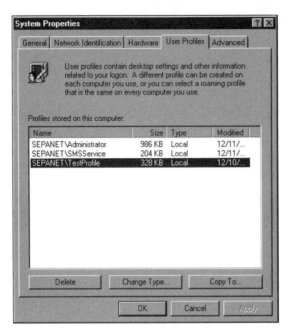

Figure 11-17 System Properties\User Profiles showing the list of profiles stored on the system

3. Log back on to Server2 using the TestProfile account. Right-click an empty section of the desktop and click **Properties**. In the Display Properties dialog box, click the **Appearance** tab. Make a note of the current color scheme.

4. Choose a new color scheme and click **OK**. The new settings will take effect immediately. Log off Server2 and then log on to Server2 again as TestProfile Note whether the settings were saved.

5. You have now created a local profile on Server2. Note whether this profile exists for domain users and note the reasons why or why not.

6. Create a new folder on Server1 under the path **C:\Profiles** and share the folder as **Profiles** with the shared folder permission of **Everyone/Full Control**.

7. Make certain that you are logged on as an Administrator on Server1 and then click **Start**, point to **Settings**, point to **Control Panel**, click **System**, and then click **User Profiles**. In the Profiles stored on this computer dialog box, click the **TestProfile** profile and click **Copy To**. In the Copy profile to box, type the path to the Server1\Profiles shared folder. The entire path should appear as: \server1\profiles\testprofile. In the Permitted to use field, click **Change**. See Figure 11-18.

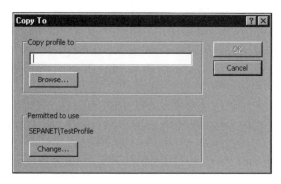

Figure 11-18   The System Profiles\Copy To dialog showing the settings to be configured

8. The Select User or Group dialog box will open. Since you want to apply these settings to all users in your corporate domain, choose **Domain Users**. Other possible choices are Authenticated Users or Everyone. Choose only one. Click **OK** twice to return to the System Properties dialog box. See Figure 11-19.

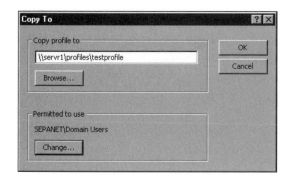

Figure 11-19   The User Profiles\Copy To dialog showing the new 'testprofile' profile

9. Click **OK** to close the System Properties dialog box.

10. To test the new desktop settings, return to Server2 and log on as any user. You should see the new desktop settings on the desktop now. Try to change the profile by changing an appearance setting and then logging off and logging on again. The requirement from Corporate Headquarters stated specifically that users must not be able to change their profiles. You will need to implement this in the lab next.

11. The previous steps created a roaming user profile. You need to create a mandatory user profile. The only difference in the steps is that the roaming user profile is named: **NTUSER.DAT**. The mandatory user profile is named: **NTUSER.MAN**. Locate the profile you created named NTUSER.DAT and change the extension from .DAT to .MAN. This is the only step required.

LAB 11.8 SUPPORTING AND IMPLEMENTING FOLDER REDIRECTION FOR WINDOWS 2000 CLIENTS

Lab Scenario

You have implemented User Profiles for your Windows NT 4.0 users. You now nee
to provide the same level of support for your Windows 2000 users. In Windows 200(
this support is obtained through the use of Folder Redirection, which is a feature c
AD GPOs. The use of User Profiles for Windows 2000 is only for those Windows 200·
users who do not belong to a domain. For domain members, this lab represents the pre
ferred implementation of this support. The constraints from the previous lab are still i:
place. Review those before beginning this lab.

Objectives

The goal of this lab is to introduce you to the general concepts of Folder Redirectio■
for Windows 2000 from AD. Folder Redirection is implemented as a GPO in AD an·
offers improved flexibility and power. After completing this lab, you will be able to:

> ➤ Design Folder Redirection GPOs for AD.

> ➤ Implement Folder Redirection at the Domain/OU level to support your users.

> ➤ Understand the advantages of Folder Redirection.

Materials Required

This lab will require the following:

> ➤ Access to two computers running Windows 2000 Server

>> ■ Server1

>> ■ Server2

> ➤ Access to the *Windows 2000 Server Resource Kit, Supplement 1*

Activity Prerequisites

Lab is to be set up as stated in the Lab Setup Guide.

ACTIVITY

In this lab you will implement a simple example of Folder Redirection. This will introduce you to the concept and allow you to experiment with the technique.

1. You will need to create a new user account in AD. Create a new OU in AD
   named **FDRUser_OU**. Create a new user account and name the account
   FDRUser. Assign a password to the account of *password*. See Figure 11-20.

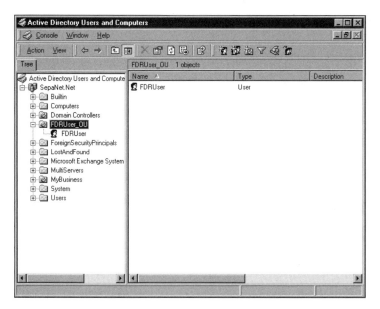

Figure 11-20   Active Directory Users and Computers showing the FDRUser OU object

2. Using Server1, log on to AD using the FDRUser account. Once you have logged on, create a new text document in the My Documents folder. Name the document **FDRUser** and then record the path to the newly created file (*C:\Documents and Settings\FDRUser\FDRUser.txt*). When you have completed these steps, log off as FDRUser and log on as Administrator.

3. On Server2, log on as administrator and create a new folder named **Redirection_Test** at the root of drive C. Share the folder as Redirection_Test and accept the default share permissions.

4. From Server1, open Active Directory Users and Computers. From the console tree view, expand the view, of your domain, right-click **FDRUser_OU**, and click the **Properties** tab.

5. In the Group Policy dialog box, click **New** and type a new group policy name of **FDRUser_OU**. Then click **Edit**. See Figure 11-21.

11

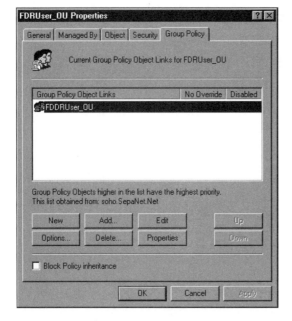

Figure 11-21   The AD FDRUser_OU object properties\group policy tab

6. Navigate to **User Configuration | Windows Settings | Folder Redirection**. Right-click **My Documents** and click **Properties**. From the pull-down menu Setting, choose the setting for **Basic – Redirect everyone's folder to the same location**. In the field Target folder location, type the path to Server2 as it was created in Step 3 above and type the additional command **%username%**. The line should resemble the following: **\\server2\redirection_test\%username%**. Then click the **Settings** tab. Examine the additional settings available here. When you have finished, click **OK**. Close the Group Policy view, close Active Directory Users and Computers, and then log off of Server1. See Figures 11-22, 11-23, and 11-24.

7. On Server 2, log off as the user FDRUser and then log on again as **FDRUser**. Note the location of the My Documents folder now for the user FDRUser. Try to move this folder to a new location and note whether you were successful.

8. Note the permissions that have been set for the FDRUser My Documents folder. Note whether the My Documents folder contains the text document that was created earlier. Log off of Server2.

9. Return to Server1 and use Active Directory Users and Computers to delete the FDRUser_OU GPO. When this has been deleted, close Active Directory Users and Computers.

10. Return to Server2 and log on again as the user FDRUser. Note the location of the Documents and Settings folder now for this user. Log off of Server2.

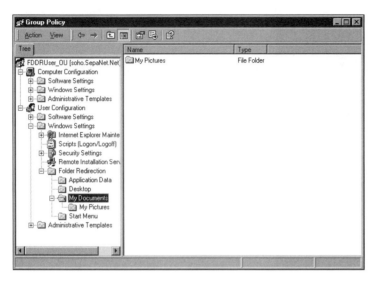

Figure 11-22   AD FDRUser_OU Group Policy Object\My Documents expanded

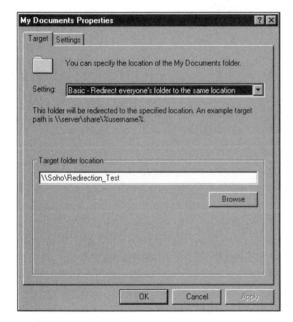

11

Figure 11-23   FDRUser_OU\My Documents Properties\Target tab showing configured settings

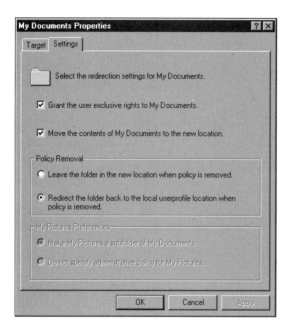

Figure 11-24   FDRUser_OU\My Documents Properties\Settings tab showing
configured settings

LAB 11.9 COMPARING AND CONTRASTING USER PROFILES AND FOLDER REDIRECTION

Lab Scenario

You have been notified that the CEO has been watching your work in securing the corporate environment. As a result, you have been called into a meeting of the Board of Directors to explain what you have implemented under the guidance and direction of the CEO. It is imperative to your future, the future of your design team, and the future of your corporate champion, the CEO, that you thoroughly understand the difference between Windows NT 4.0-style User Profiles and Windows 2000 Folder Redirection. You will need to answer questions posed by the members of the Board of Directors. You will need to be able to explain in detail the differences in the two concepts. You have asked and received permission from the CEO to bring members of your design team into the meeting to more fully participate in the process. Do your research carefully. Be prepared to explain the differences and advantages, if any, of each technique and the operating systems that each method supports.

Objectives

The goal of this lab is to compare and contrast User Profiles and Group Policy. This is an instructor-led, role-playing lab. You and the other students are encouraged to make this lab as realistic as possible. The instructor will assign roles for each participant and outline specific levels of computer knowledge for students playing the roles of members of the Board. The members of the Board should prepare by creating realistic questions for the design team. Students playing the part of design team members should be well prepared.

After completing this lab, you will be able to:

➤ Fully explain the differences between User Profiles and Group Policy.

➤ Appreciate the finer points that distinguish User Profiles from Group Policies.

➤ Explain what kind of user/computer should use User Profiles and what kind of user/computer should use Group Policies.

➤ Understand the implementation details of each.

Materials Required

This lab will require the following:

➤ Access to the *Windows 2000 Server Resource Kit, Supplement 1*

➤ Paper, pens

➤ Whiteboard or chalkboard

➤ Full participation from all students

Activity Prerequisites

Lab is to be set up as stated in the Lab Setup Guide.

ACTIVITY

Answer questions from the Corporation's Board of Directors supporting the CEO's decision to allow this level of AD implementation.

CHAPTER TWELVE

DEPLOYING AND MANAGING SOFTWARE USING GROUP POLICY

Labs included in this chapter

➤ Lab 12.1 Computer Management Concepts and Total Cost of Ownership

➤ Lab 12.2 IntelliMirror

➤ Lab 12.3 Software Management Phases

➤ Lab 12.4 Creating and Configuring Windows Installer Packages for Windows 2000 and Down-level Clients

➤ Lab 12.5 Using GPOs to Manage and Install WinINSTALL LE Packages

➤ Lab 12.6 Using the Software Installation Snap-in

➤ Lab 12.7 Assigned Applications versus Published Applications

➤ Lab 12.8 Patching and Updating Software Using WinINSTALL LE

Microsoft MCSE Exam #70-217 Objectives	
Objective	Lab
Configuring, Managing, Monitoring, Optimizing, and Troubleshooting Change and Configuration Management	12.1, 12.4, 12.5, 12.7, 12.8

179

LAB 12.1 COMPUTER MANAGEMENT CONCEPTS AND TOTAL COST OF OWNERSHIP

Lab Scenario

One of the most important benefits of Active Directory is its ability to improve computer management and allow a corporation to lower the corporate Total Cost of Ownership (TCO) by controlling software installation and distribution. The two companies that you support, Thisbin Co. and Kronk Design, would now like to apply AD GPOs to reap the benefits of reduced TCO. Both companies have past histories of free and unrestricted computer software installation by their employees. Many employees have downloaded software from the Internet without purchasing the proper licenses. Some employees have purchased software at various retail outlets and then installed this software on their machines at work. Others have loaned installation media to their co-workers and allowed them to install the software a second time, in direct violation of the license. Your corporate legal staff has done some research and informed the owners that this policy is a ticking time bomb. The old policy has resulted in significant downtime and a loss of some revenue. Additionally, the BSA (Business Software Alliance, http://www.bsa.org/usa/) has become active in your area and is looking for companies who are violating computer software licenses. They have Federal enforcement power and could shut down the business if they found pirated or illegal software installed. Recently a large company was forced to pay a fine of $4.5 million dollars for having unlicensed software on their computers. The owners are very anxious that this not happen to either Thisbin Co. or Kronk Designs.

The owners have decided to address this situation in both companies. You and your design team have been assigned to research and design a series of GPOs for enforcing software management and control within the organizations. Your ultimate goal is to reduce TCO to the lowest level possible.

Objectives

Your goal in this lab is to begin the process of planning your implementation of TCO reduction for your employer. Based on material gathered from previous labs, and the results and implementations from those labs, you will arrive at a design for appropriate GPOs to implement in your AD structure. After completing this lab, you will be able to:

➤ Design and implement GPOs to control and enhance TCO benefits.

➤ Redesign AD to afford better implementation of the TCO benefits.

➤ Understand the TCO Reduction Discovery process.

➤ Design the appropriate GPOs to enforce software control for both users and their computers.

Materials Required

This lab will require the following:

➤ Access to *Windows 2000 Server Resource Kit, Supplement 1*

➤ Access to a Windows 2000 Server with Active Directory installed

➤ Your planning documents from previous labs

➤ Paper, pen, pencils, and/or a whiteboard

Activity Prerequisites

Lab is to be set up as stated in the Lab Setup Guide.

ACTIVITY

You will need to determine effective settings to be applied in the GPOs, with your central focus being administrative cost reduction and minimization of downtime due to incorrect software configuration and/or installation. You will need to make some decisions that will not be popular with many users, but that will satisfy the requirements of the owners.

Your first steps should be to examine the range of options that are available to you for controlling the users' work environment. To determine these options, complete the steps below.

1. Open Active Directory Users and Computers and choose one of the OUs that you created in a previous lab. You should see something similar to Figure 12-1.

12

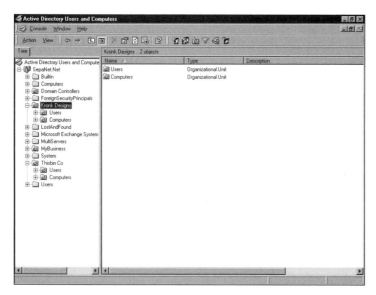

Figure 12-1   AD Users and Computers, Thisbin Co. and Kronk Designs OU implementation

2. Expand one of these OUs, then click **Properties** and click the **Group Policy** tab. You may see something similar to Figure 12-2. If you do not see a GPO on this screen, create one so you will be able to complete this section.

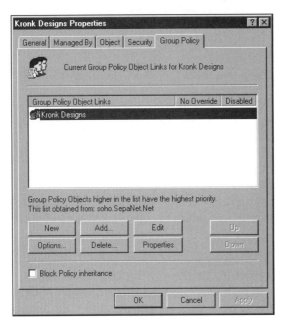

Figure 12-2   Kronk Designs AD GPO for software installation

3. Highlight the GPO and click **Edit**. This will direct you to the next screen. To reach the first area of interest, click **Computer Configuration**, point to **Software Settings**, and click **Software Installation**. To reach the second area of interest, click **User Configuration**, point to **Software Settings**, and click **Software Installation**. See Figure 12-3.

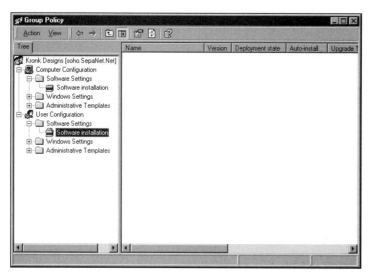

Figure 12-3   Kronk Designs User Software settings for GPOs

4. This is the primary area of interest for controlling software installation and management. You can see that two kinds of software installation are provided, one under the Computer Configuration tree and a second under the User Configuration tree. See Figures 12-4 and 12-5.

12

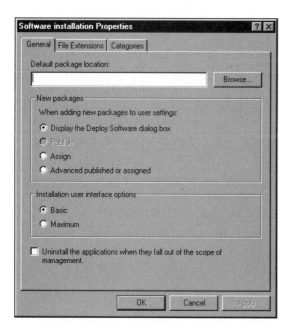

Figure 12-4   The GPO Software Installation Configuration page showing some possible settings for Assigned Software

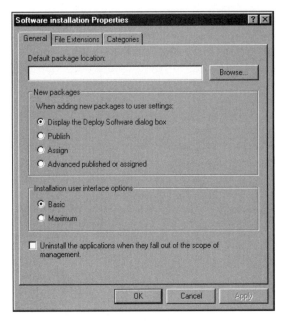

Figure 12-5   The GPO Software Installation Configuration page showing some possible settings for published software

5. Examine the two illustrations above carefully.

   a. Do you see any differences between the tools?

   b. What differences are you seeing?

   c. Explain the differences.

6. Close AD Users and Computers.

7. Now make a list of software that needs to be supported in your corporate environment. You will need to differentiate between different kinds of software. As a starting point:

   a. Make a first list of all software that meets these criteria:

      i.   Required on all computers, regardless of who the computer belongs to

      ii. Cannot be uninstalled by the users

      iii. Cannot be substantially modified by the users

      iv. Is subject to mandatory updates or new data file installations

   b. Make a second list of all software that meets these criteria:

      i.   May not be required by all users; may be optional for some or not required at all for others

      ii. Supports selective, optional installation by the users

      iii. Can be uninstalled by the users or through another process

      iv. Is subject to optional updates or new data file installations

8. Once you have created these two lists, begin formulating the distribution of the respective software packages inside your AD implementation. You may redesign/redistribute users, their computers, or OUs if you can justify the need to do so. You may not spend any company funds at this point beyond incidental, normal expenses.

LAB 12.2 INTELLIMIRROR

Lab Scenario

What is IntelliMirror? What can it do for you in the role of supporting Thisbin Co. and Kronk Design? IntelliMirror is a technology used in AD to allow administrators to make use of policy-based regulation of all aspects of a user's computer. This control extends from the startup scripts applied to the machine, to the logon scripts applied to the user, to the applications the user is allowed to run or use. IntelliMirror is comprised of three different functionalities. They are:

➤ User Data Management

➤ User Setting Management

➤ Software Installation and Management

You have already used two of these functions in your environment, namely User Data Management and User Setting Management. It is now time to apply the third function, Software Installation and Management, to Thisbin Co. and Kronk Designs.

Objectives

The goal of this planning lab is to build upon the information collected in Lab 12.1, and to formulate your policy for software support using AD GPOs and the IntelliMirror technologies. What software is already installed in your environment? How many different types of anti-virus software are in place in your organization? What kinds of e-mail clients are used? Have you standardized on a web browser? Do your users have software from home installed on their computers? If so, do they have licenses for the software? Have you investigated the use of a software auditing tool in your environment? Such a tool is available, free of charge after registration, for a 60-day evaluation from the BSA. This would be a good start. After completing this lab, you will be able to:

➤ Understand the reason for a software audit looking for non-compliant software.

➤ Implement a software standards process.

➤ Conform to the software licensing standards as put forth by the BSA.

➤ Develop a plan for dealing with illegal software.

➤ Formulate actions for users who persist in trying to use illegal software.

Materials Required

This lab will require the following:

➤ Access to *Windows 2000 Server Resource Kit, Supplement 1*

➤ Access to a Windows 2000 Server with Active Directory installed

➤ Your planning documents from previous labs

➤ An opportunity to examine/visit the BSA web site

➤ Paper, pen, pencils, and/or a whiteboard

Activity Prerequisites

Lab is to be set up as stated in the Lab Setup Guide.

ACTIVITY

Assemble your design team and assign roles and responsibilities to each team member. Make a determination of what software should be installed on each desktop. What licenses are required and do any applications allow the use of the software in two different locations, provided that both machines are not running at the same time? Are all of your OSs licensed correctly? If using MS Windows 2000 Terminal Server, do you have the appropriate licenses for the clients? Have a team member investigate software auditing tools and report back to your team on their findings. Involve management and arrive at a corporate policy for dealing with users who persist in using or trying to install unlicensed software. Also, in the event the BSA should arrive to check your software compliance, how will you respond? Do you have all of your licenses on site? Are they all located in one place, or scattered throughout the building? For your users who have their own software installed, can they produce the licenses on short (one hour) notice? Investigate all possibilities and be prepared to explain and justify your findings to the class.

LAB 12.3 SOFTWARE MANAGEMENT PHASES

Lab Scenario

You have investigated, you have formulated, and you have started to plan. The time has come to take action. The *Microsoft Windows 2000 Server Resource Kit, Supplement 1, Part 4,*

Chapter 23, page 1296 identifies four separate phases of software deployment. The four phases are summarized below:

Table 12-1   Software Management Phases

Phase	Process
Preparation	Analysis of software needs and collection/creation of Windows Installer (msi) packages required for installation
Distribution	Creation of network distribution points for installation, and assurance that desired software is available for installation
Scope of Management	Determination of relevant software loads for employees
Installation Options	Configuration of software deployment options, modifications, and/or whether software is to be repaired or removed

The first phase of the four management phases has been completed. You have analyzed the corporate needs and requirements, and you have started to collect the required software and licenses. You have presented the results of your preliminary survey to management and received their approval. You have performed your corporate software compliance audit and have taken appropriate actions based on those findings. The next steps in the process are laid out in the table above, and you now need to prepare for them.

Objectives

The goal of this lab is to determine whether your infrastructure can support the process. You need to know this before you begin the process of actually implementing your GPO-based software management policies. After completing this lab, you will be able to:

➤ Complete the design phase of GPO-based software deployment.

➤ Integrate the results of a corporate software audit into the planning process for your deployment.

➤ Make a determination of who should receive specific applications and who should not receive those applications.

➤ Formulate procedures for individual deviation (if any) from corporate standards.

➤ Formulate responses for unauthorized individual deviations from the approved corporate software policy.

➤ Formulate a procedure to be used in the event of an unannounced audit by the BSA.

➤ Centralize the storage of all corporate software licenses.

Materials Required

This lab will require the following:

➤ Access to *Windows 2000 Server Resource Kit, Supplement 1*

➤ Access to a Windows 2000 Server with Active Directory installed

➤ Your planning documents from previous labs

➤ Paper, pen, pencils, and/or a whiteboard

Activity Prerequisites

Lab is to be set up as stated in the Lab Setup Guide.

ACTIVITY

This is a planning exercise. Assign specific roles and duties to the members of your design team. Consider the following questions.

Since this is a network-based process, is your infrastructure capable of supporting this technology? Do you have servers that can support the software distribution points associated with the process? Have you determined who will be receiving specific software loads? Will software be installed on a machine basis? Will it be installed on a user basis? Or will you employ a combination of both techniques? Will software be installed against specific OUs within the corporate structure? Is there one specific application that needs to be applied to both Thisbin Com. and Kronk Designs, or are there specific applications that should be applied to only one company and not the other?

Once this is done, use the bulleted list above to complete the exercise. Remember that the design of each team will be different. At the conclusion of the lab, present your solution to the rest of the class. Be prepared to justify all of your design decisions. As a condition of this lab, you have received permission to spend whatever monies are necessary in order to bring both companies, Thisbin Co. and Kronk Designs, into full, complete compliance with BSA guidelines for the licensing of software. When you have completed this lab, you will begin the process of actually creating MSI files and configuring the installation options.

LAB 12.4 CREATING AND CONFIGURING WINDOWS INSTALLER PACKAGES FOR WINDOWS 2000 AND DOWN-LEVEL CLIENTS

Lab Scenario

It is now time to begin the process of creating MSI packages for your GPO-based software installations. If you have made the decision to use new applications from Microsoft, it will be unnecessary to create MSI files as all new Microsoft applications have MSI files already on the installation media. The MSI creation process is for applications that are from third parties, which did not provide MSI files on their media, and for older applications that were written before the advent of the MSI technology.

You have been able to purchase all new software for Thisbin Co., and most of the software for Kronk Designs is also new, current software. However, Kronk Designs also has a few users who use **Borland PASCAL with Objects 7.0** for certain key business functions. This application is on 10, 3.5″ floppy disks and you are no longer able to purchase replacement media. It is imperative that this application be transferred over to an MSI technology because:

> ➤ It is not practical to pass floppies around for installation of the software.

> ➤ This is the only set of floppies that you have.

> ➤ This is a key business application that Kronk Designs refuses to replace.

Objectives

You and your design team have several tasks to complete during this lab. Since you have already decided to implement the MSI technology, there is very little planning to be done. This particular job involves the implementation of the MSI technology and tools on two computers in your environment. *Server1* will serve as the target machine. It is imperative that this machine does not have a current or past installation of the intended application. For performance issues and for the purposes of guaranteeing a clean build process in the real world, it is recommended that this machine be a fresh, clean installation of the desired target OS (Windows 2000 Server in this case). This machine should have any and all required service packs installed and should be representative of all target machines in terms of directory structure and partition mappings. The second machine will be the host for the WinINSTALL LE program and needs sufficient hard drive space to hold the MSI files that will be generated during the processing. Both machines require network connectivity. An advantage would be their placement on an isolated network segment, free of traffic from other machines.

12

The MSI process is not a true software installation, but rather an imaging of the HD with the desired file structure and a reconfiguration of the system registry to reflect an actual installation of the application. Both of these events, the construction of the directory structure and the modification of the system registry to reflect the installation, actually take place on the target machine during the MSI creation process. After completing this lab, you will be able to:

> ➤ Install WinINSTALL LE and configure the application for capture.

> ➤ Understand the MSI creation process and method.

> ➤ Know how to configure the target and host machines for the process.

> ➤ Know how to perform advance configuration of the target machine for generation of the MSI file.

> ➤ Complete the MSI process.

Materials Required

This lab will require the following:

> ➤ Access to *Windows 2000 Server Resource Kit, Supplement 1*

➤ Access to Windows 2000 Server installation media

➤ Access to two Windows 2000 servers with Active Directory installed

- Server1

- Server2

➤ Your planning documents from previous labs

➤ A non-Microsoft application to use for testing purposes

Activity Prerequisites

Lab is to be set up as stated in the Lab Setup Guide.

ACTIVITY

Complete the steps listed below on Server2, which will serve as the Host for WinINSTALL LE during the lab.

1. Navigate to the path **CD_DRIVE\VALUEADD\3RDPARTY\MGMT\ WINSTLE**. You will find the WinINSTALL LE installation file here. The file is named SWIADMLE.MSI, as shown in Figure 12-6. Double-click this file to begin the installation process.

Figure 12-6   The installation path for the WinINSTALL LE tool on the installation media

2. You will see the screen in Figure 12-7 during the installation process. When this screen closes, the software has been installed. No reboot is necessary.

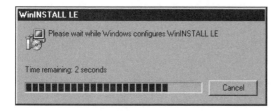

Figure 12-7   The WinINSTALL LE message telling you to wait while your software is configured

3. Figure 12-8 shows the new application that will appear on your **Programs | VERITAS Software | VERITAS Discover** and **Programs | VERITAS Software | VERITAS Software Console**.

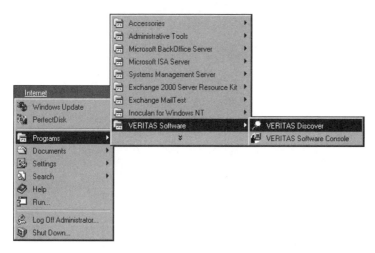

Figure 12-8   The menu listings for VERITAS software, the makers of WinINSTALL LE tool

4. Opening the VERITAS Software Console will show this tool console. See Figure 12-9. Right-click **Windows Installer Package Editor** and click **Open** to open an MSI file. Use the Adminpak.MSI file located in the System 32 directory to open and examine the contents of an MSI package.

Figure 12-9   The WinINSTALL LE main console waiting for a task

5. Expand the path shown in Figure 12-10 on your machine to explore the contents of an MSI file. You do not need to configure these settings. The WinINSTALL LE application will configure them for you. Also be sure to examine the top-level path of the MSI for additional customization information stored there. See Figure 12-11.

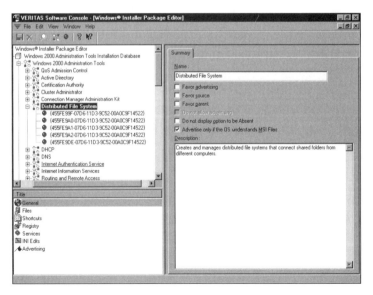

Figure 12-10   The contents of ADMINPAK.MSI expanded using WinINSTALL LE

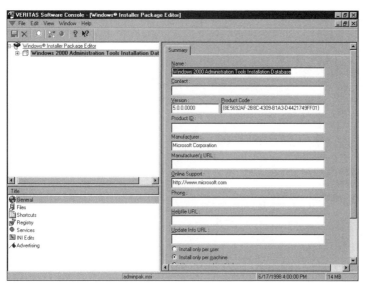

Figure 12-11   Additional properties for WinINSTALL LE

6. On Server2, locate the folder named WinINSTALL, which is in the path **Drive:\Program Files\VERITAS Software**, and create a share on the folder. The next steps will take place on the target machine, Server1.

7. On Server1, run the program named **DISCOZ.EXE** from the host machine.

12

Do not map a drive to this folder.

8. The dialog box that you will see is shown in Figure 12-12.

Figure 12-12   The WinINSTALL LE Discover tool running in its first pass through the system

9. Click **Next** to continue the process. Fill in the fields on the next screen, as shown in Figure 12-13.

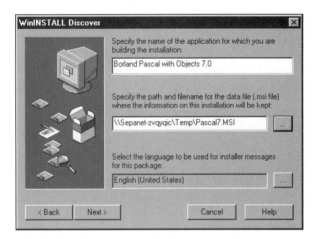

Figure 12-13   The WinINSTALL LE tool creating a new application

10. Click **Next** to continue and accept the default locations for the storage of temporary files. Choose a drive to scan for changes and then click **Next**. See Figures 12-14 and 12-15.

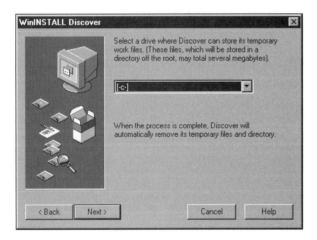

Figure 12-14   A WinINSTALL LE configuration screen

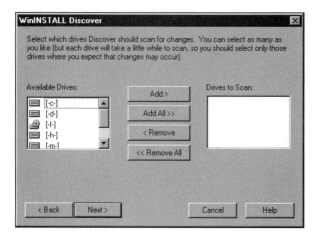

Figure 12-15   The WinINSTALL LE drive mapping field

> 11. Configure the WinINSTALL LE Discover tool as shown in Figure 12-16 and proceed.

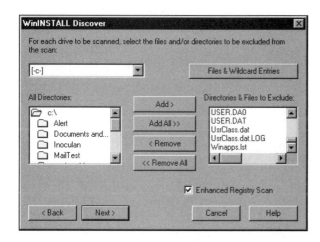

Figure 12-16   The WinINSTALL LE file mapping utility

WinINSTALL LE is now scanning your drives and taking a snapshot of the machine state prior to the installation of the new software application. Allow the process to continue until completion. See Figure 12-17.

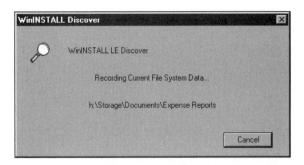

Figure 12-17   WinINSTALL LE scanning the registry prior to installing software

12. After the first stage finishes, you will see the message shown in Figure 12-18. Click **OK** to proceed.

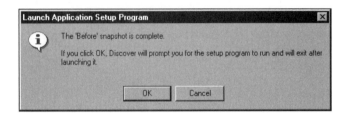

Figure 12-18   WinINSTALL LE has finished its first pass

13. In the Run Application Setup Program dialog box, shown in Figure 12-19, choose the name of your installation file and proceed with a normal installation of the program.

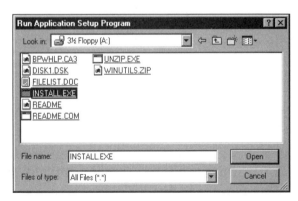

Figure 12-19   Selecting the new application setup file

14. In this particular case, the install screen looks like Figure 12-20.

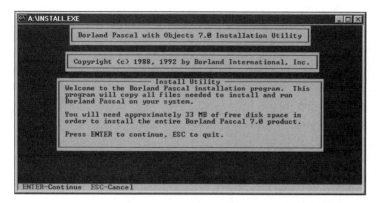

Figure 12-20   The first installation screen for Borland Turbo Pascal 7.0

15. Make certain to configure the application installation as you wish it to exist on all computers to receive the MSI file. Remember, this is not a true installation being prepared; it is very similar to a drive image on a smaller scale. It is in fact a folder image process. See Figure 12-21.

Figure 12-21   The configuration options menu for installing Turbo Pascal

16. After the installation is complete, you will need to restart the target computer in order to finalize any Registry modifications. This is not an optional step. Following the restart, you will again run the WinINSTALL LE Discover tool to detect Registry modifications. Click **Start**, point to **Programs**, click **VERITAS Software**, and then click **VERITAS Software Discover**.

17. Now that your target computer, Server1, has restarted, run the WinINSTALL LE Discover tool again to record changes made to the system registry. You will see the screen shown in Figure 12-22.

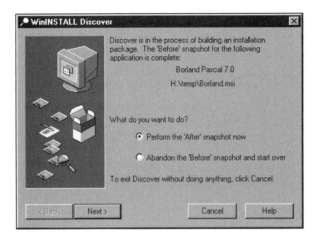

Figure 12-22   The third step in the MSI process

18. Click **Next**. WinINSTALL LE is now checking for changes to the system registry. If any error messages appear, choose the Ignore option to bypass these messages. When the entire process has finished, you will see the message shown in Figure 12-23.

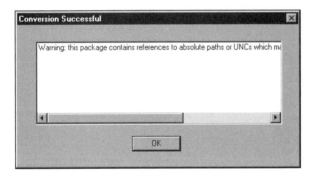

Figure 12-23   Your conversation to MSI was successful

19. Click **OK** to continue. The message indicating a successful completion is shown in Figure 12-24.

Figure 12-24   The MSI completion message

20. Figure 12-25 shows the properties page for the Borland.msi file.

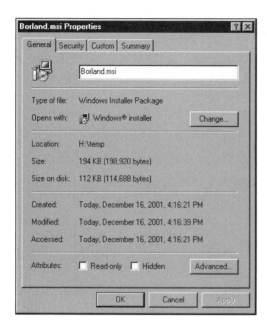

Figure 12-25   An MSI installation configuration screen

21. Figure 12-26 shows a screen shot of the finished product.

12

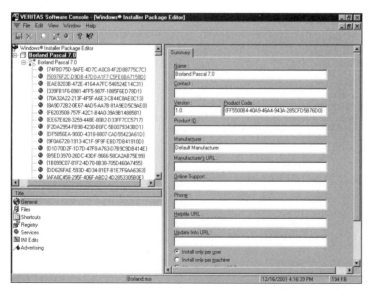

Figure 12-26   Some of the contents of the Borland MSI file showing details

22. The lab is now complete. You should have an understanding of how to create basic MSI files.

LAB 12.5 USING GPOs TO MANAGE AND INSTALL WinINSTALL LE PACKAGES

Lab Scenario

Now that you have created your MSI applications and have obtained licenses for the installation of these copies of the application, the rest of your work is easy. You now need to configure AD GPOs to support the installation of your software. Thisbin Co. and Kronk Designs have provided some specifics for you. You and your team need to config ure your installation policy to support these specifics.

Objectives

The goal in this lab is to configure GPOs to support the installation of software using MSI files. Your employers, Thisbin Co. and Kronk Designs, have mandated certain behav iors for specific software classes. These behaviors are:

> ➤ Antivirus software will be installed on all machines, regardless of who the user is. This is a mandatory installation. Individual variance will not be tolerated.

> ➤ Common desktops will be in place for all computers, regardless of who the user is. This is a mandatory installation. Individual variance will not be tolerated.

> ➤ Specific software applications will be installed for specific workgroups. All users will no longer receive the entire installation from the MS Office Suite. All users will receive:

>> ▪ A corporate e-mail client

>> ▪ A word processor

>> ▪ A web browser

> ➤ Additional applications will be installed only if that user's manager signs off on the installation of the requested application.

Your job and the job of your team will be to design the GPOs to support these goals. You are not to actually use the tools to configure the GPOs yet. You will apply the GPO on the basis of Forest, Domain, and OU membership, making informed decisions con cerning the correct placement and implementation of the GPOs based upon the struc ture of the AD Forest. You may not redesign AD. You must use the structure you currently have from your previous planning exercises. After completing this lab, you will be able to:

> ➤ Design the implementation of GPOs for supporting software.

> ➤ Apply these designs to an AD OU structure.

> ➤ Plan your software GPOs to support your AD design.

Materials Required

This lab will require the following:

➤ Access to *Windows 2000 Server Resource Kit, Supplement 1*

➤ Access to a Windows 2000 Server with Active Directory installed

➤ Your planning documents from previous labs

➤ Paper, pen, pencils, and/or a whiteboard

Activity Prerequisites

Lab is to be set up as stated in the Lab Setup Guide.

ACTIVITY

As a planning exercise, the steps involved should be second nature to you now. Create your plan. Be prepared to explain your plan to your classmates. Make sure to fully utilize all members of your design team.

LAB 12.6 USING THE SOFTWARE INSTALLATION SNAP-IN

Lab Scenario

You are now ready to begin the creation of your software GPOs. Corporate has signed off on your designs and given you the go-ahead. For ease of creation, you are in the office on Saturday morning so that you may reconfigure your environment and test your settings without the users interfering in the process.

Objectives

You will implement your AD GPOs for software deployment using the appropriate tools and techniques. You will need to create new GPOs as needed at the required levels and configure the correct policies. Remember, this exercise is to be used to configure only software installation options. You may not modify other parts of your AD implementation. After completing this lab, you will be able to:

➤ Use the GPO tool to create software GPOs.

➤ Assign the correct level of access to those GPOs.

Materials Required

This lab will require the following:

➤ Access to *Windows 2000 Server Resource Kit, Supplement 1*

➤ Access to a Windows 2000 Server with Active Directory installed

➤ Your planning documents from previous labs

12

Activity Prerequisites

Lab is to be set up as stated in the Lab Setup Guide.

ACTIVITY

1. Open Active Directory Users and Computers and choose the relevant level of object. If you are applying software for the entire domain, then choose a domain. If you are applying the software for an OU, then choose that OU.

2. Right-click the object. Click **Properties**, and click **Group Policy**. Then click **New** and enter the name of the new GPO. See Figure 12-27.

3. Click the **Edit** button to proceed to the Group Policy snap-in tool. Choose either **Computer Configuration\Software Settings** or **User Configuration\Software Settings**, and then right-click **Software installation**. Click **New**, click **Package**, and then type the path to your installation files.

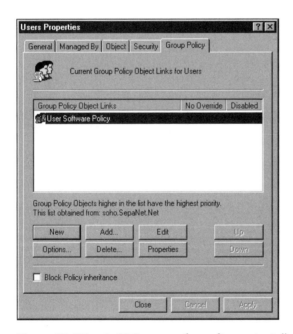

Figure 12-27 A GPO screen for software installation

Be sure to type a path to a network share. Entering a local path here will produce an error when the GPO tries to run.

4. Continue the configuration process, exploring the additional settings.

5. Repeat this process for any additional GPOs that need to be configured.

6. When you are finished, compare your results with your classmates' to view their solutions.

LAB 12.7 ASSIGNED APPLICATIONS VERSUS PUBLISHED APPLICATIONS

Lab Scenario

You have designed your GPOs but they do not seem to be working as intended. The installations seem to be haphazard, with some users not receiving any GPOs and others receiving too many. You may need to re-examine your settings and reconfigure. Remember that GPO-based software installation supports two different modes of operation. The first mode is Assigned Applications. Applications that have been assigned are assigned for all computers, regardless of what user is sitting at that computer. The second mode is Published Applications. Applications that are published are available to all users who have the correct permissions in AD to see the programs. In order for Application Publishing to work as a software catalog for the users, you must be certain to not remove the Control Panel applet Add or Remove Programs through another GPO. Applications that have been assigned exist as an icon on the desktop and are not actually installed until the user triggers them. Published applications can be available as applications listed in a software catalog or can be activated by the user triggering their installation by clicking on an unknown file format. A user could, for instance, receive a PowerPoint attachment from another user and click the attachment to open it. The act of opening the slide show will trigger the installation of PowerPoint. With these facts in mind, continue.

12

Objectives

If you need to reconfigure your GPOs, you need to make some decisions. Which software settings are to be applied only against computers and which settings are to be applied only against users? In addition, are there any software applications that should be made available to the users following approval by their managers? How will you deploy these packages? Reformulate your deployment plans and continue. After completing this lab, you will be able to:

➤ Distinguish between Published applications and Assigned applications.

➤ Understand the implementation of each.

➤ Understand the implications of each.

Materials Required

This lab will require the following:

➤ Access to *Windows 2000 Server Resource Kit, Supplement 1*

➤ Access to a Windows 2000 Server with Active Directory installed

➤ Your planning documents from previous labs

Activity Prerequisites

Lab is to be set up as stated in the Lab Setup Guide.

ACTIVITY

Revisit your GPO design for software installation and make any necessary corrections to implement your desired policies correctly. Test your new settings for proper functionality. Experiment with other settings to understand the full power of the IntelliMirror-based GPO software installation tools.

LAB 12.8 PATCHING AND UPDATING SOFTWARE USING WININSTALL LE

Lab Scenario

You have successfully applied your GPO-based software installations and everything seems to be working well. However, your antivirus application is constantly being updated with new drivers and you have also received the new Service Pack for Windows 2000. You would like to install these patches and updates using your IntelliMirror GPO because currently you are performing manual updates of these files, particularly the Service Pack files. This is a very time-consuming process for your support staff. Is there an alternative available to you? How can you modify your current GPOs to support this technique? Additionally, can you configure your GPOs to remove software from the client computers when company policy dictates such removal?

Objectives

Your goal in this planning lab is to investigate the possibilities of fully automating your software configuration processes beyond the installation of new software. After completing this lab, you will be able to:

➤ Implement an unattended update process.

➤ Automate the installation of patches and updates using IntelliMirror GPOs.

➤ Configure GPOs to remove software.

Materials Required

➤ Access to *Windows 2000 Server Resource Kit, Supplement 1*

➤ Access to a Windows 2000 server with Active Directory installed

➤ Your planning documents from previous labs

Activity Prerequisites

Lab is to be set up as stated in the Lab Setup Guide.

ACTIVITY

Design the standards and procedures that you will implement to support the unattended update process for currently installed software applications and suites in your environment. Make certain to include planning for any antivirus applications in use in your corporate infrastructure. Also, examine the techniques for deploying Service Packs for both Windows 2000 and down-level clients. You are to automate this process as much as possible through your GPO designs. If possible, test your configuration in the lab to determine whether it is effective.

Investigate the options available in AD for applying Service Packs. Try to configure your GPOs to remove old software. Configure a GPO to remove software when the user moves from the scope of management. Can your GPOs be configured to remove software installed by the user in favor of software owned by the corporation and so eliminate one possible source of software license violation? As a planning lab, assemble your design team and investigate your options, using role-playing to fully explore all possibilities. Be prepared to present your solution/findings in front of the class. Assume that these are your managers and employers you are presenting to, not your classmates. Be prepared to justify your implementations.

12

DEPLOYING WINDOWS 2000 USING REMOTE INSTALLATION SERVICES

Labs included in this chapter

➤ Lab 13.1 How RIS Functions

➤ Lab 13.2 Configuring Active Directory and Network Services for Supporting RIS

➤ Lab 13.3 Determining Client and Server Requirements for RIS

➤ Lab 13.4 Configuring RIS Using RISetup

➤ Lab 13.5 Creating RIS Images

➤ Lab 13.6 Creating and Troubleshooting RIS Boot Disks

➤ Lab 13.7 Managing RIS Security

➤ Lab 13.8 Troubleshooting the RIS Process

Microsoft MCSE Exam #70-217 Objectives	
Objective	Lab
Installing and Configuring Active Directory	13.1, 13.2, 13.4, 13.5
Installing, Configuring, Managing, Monitoring, and Troubleshooting DNS for Active Directory	13.2, 13.3
Configuring, Managing, Monitoring, Optimizing, and Troubleshooting Change and Configuration Management	13.1, 13.2, 13.3, 13.4, 13.5, 13.6, 13.7, 13.8
Configuring, Managing, Monitoring, and Troubleshooting Security in a Directory Services Infrastructure	13.1, 13.2, 13.7, 13.8

LAB 13.1 HOW RIS FUNCTIONS

Lab Scenario

The owners of the companies that you support, Thisbin Co. and Kronk Design approached you about further optimization of your IT infrastructure. One of the techniques you are investigating is Remote Installation Services (RIS). Upon further investigation, you realize that RIS would indeed be a very valuable technique for your infrastructure.

Objectives

The goal of this lab is to automate as much of the day-to-day infrastructure support as possible to provide enhanced functionality for your infrastructure. In addition, you would like a secure implementation for your environment to avoid the possibility of users disrupting your setup. You will need to investigate the power and functionality of RIS. After completing this lab, you will be able to:

> ➤ Use RIS for automated deployment of client workstations.

> ➤ Use RIS for automated deployment of servers, including AD Servers.

> ➤ Support automated installation of applications beyond the flexibility afforded by the IntelliMirror GPO technologies.

> ➤ Provide fast, automated recovery of corrupted/infected workstations.

> ➤ Put into practice a secure implementation to prevent unauthorized RIS installations.

Materials Required

This lab will require the following:

> ➤ Access to *Windows 2000 Server Resource Kit, Supplement 1*

> ➤ Access to a Windows 2000 Server with AD installed

Activity Prerequisites

Lab is to be set up as stated in the Lab Setup Guide.

ACTIVITY

For this lab, answer the questions below, using the Server Resource Kit and having access to a Windows 2000 Server with Active Directory installed. This lab can be completed either individually or as a team project.

1. What is RIS?

2. What Active Directory components are required in order for RIS to function?

3. What operating systems are supported by RIS?

4. Is it possible to install a Windows 2000 Active Directory domain controller using RIS?

5. Is RIS a cloning technology or an unattended installation technology?

6. A network administrator configures RIS in her environment to enable workstation deployment. However, she is concerned about the possibility of users bringing laptops or workstations from home on the weekends and using her corporate build for their own machines. What can she do to prevent this from happening?

7. Can the administrator combine RIS techniques with GPOs to provide a more flexible installation process?

8. What is PXE?

9. Is Microsoft DHCP required for RIS?

LAB 13.2 CONFIGURING ACTIVE DIRECTORY AND NETWORK SERVICES FOR SUPPORTING RIS

Lab Scenario

You have decided to implement RIS in your AD environment for your two corporate customers, Thisbin Co. and Kronk Designs. You have configured your users in their respective OUs and are pleased with the functionality that you have achieved. Your automated GPOs for software deployment are also functioning correctly.

13

Objectives

The goal of this lab is to determine what network configuration settings need to be implemented in your environment in order to make RIS function correctly. After completing this lab, you will be able to:

➤ Determine the correct network configuration settings for implementing RIS.

➤ Determine RIS components to be installed into AD for functionality.

➤ Redesign AD OUs, if necessary, to implement RIS for AD security and efficiency.

➤ Analyze RIS implementations for functionality.

Materials Required

This lab will require the following:

➤ Access to *Windows 2000 Server Resource Kit, Supplement 1*

➤ Access to a Windows 2000 Server with AD installed

Activity Prerequisites

Lab is to be set up as stated in the Lab Setup Guide.

ACTIVITY

You have implemented AD with a single forest and two domains. You have create numerous OUs for the users. You have also created several large OUs for the user com puters and servers.

Using this information and the resources available to you in your lab environmen research and answer the questions below to develop your understanding of RIS as imple mented in AD.

1. Does RIS require a specific version of DNS?

2. What specific setup requirements must be applied to the NBNS service?

3. Are GPOs required for the RIS process?

4. Under what conditions can RIS be installed on a standalone Windows 2000 server?

5. You have been directed by your manager to install and configure RIS on a Windows NT 4.0 server. Explain the process in detail.

6. What version of BIND will support RIS?

7. RFCs (Request for Comments) define the standards used in network technologies. What does RFC 2136 refer to?

8. What configuration parameters must be adjusted on a Microsoft Windows 2000 WINS server?

9. When would you use an installation boot floppy?

10. What is the minimal version of PXE required for RIS functionality?

11. Is Active Directory required to implement RIS?

12. Can RIS be used to deploy other operating systems besides Windows 2000?

13. What additional services must be configured to enable RIS to function in a NetBIOS environment?

LAB 13.3 DETERMINING CLIENT AND SERVER REQUIREMENTS FOR RIS

Lab Scenario

Now that you have determined that RIS will function in your environment, you need to determine whether your servers and clients have the hardware in place to support RIS. This process is vital because you have been given the authority to upgrade your network services and computers (clients only) to fully implement RIS in your corporate environment.

Objectives

Microsoft has compiled a list of minimum hardware requirements for supporting RIS on both servers and clients. The goal of this lab will be to use this information to survey your corporate environment and determine its suitability for a RIS implementation. After completing this lab, you will be able to:

➤ Determine the minimum hardware requirements for servers to support RIS.

➤ Determine the minimum hardware requirements for clients to support RIS.

Materials Required

This lab will require the following:

➤ Access to *Windows 2000 Server Resource Kit, Supplement 1*

➤ Access to a Windows 2000 Server with AD installed

Activity Prerequisites

Lab is to be set up as stated in the Lab Setup Guide.

ACTIVITY

Use the tables below to conduct a hardware audit of your corporate servers and clients (classroom machines) to determine their suitability for RIS.

Windows 2000 Server

➤ Pentium or Pentium II 200 MHz (Pentium 166 MHz minimum)

➤ 96 to 128 MB RAM

➤ 2 GB hard disk

➤ 10 MBps NIC (100 MBps recommended)

➤ CD-ROM or access to a network share containing the correct operating system

Windows 2000 Professional

➤ Pentium 166 MHz

➤ Net PC PXE-based remote boot

➤ 32 MB RAM (64 MB RAM recommended)

➤ 800 MB hard disk

➤ DHCP PXE-based boot ROM version 0.99c or later or a NIC supported by the Windows 2000 RIS boot disk

13

Record your results below, making certain to record the specific name of each machine to avoid confusion later.

Windows 2000 Server

_____

_____

_____

_____

_____

Windows 2000 Professional

_____

_____

_____

_____

_____

LAB 13.4 CONFIGURING RIS USING RISETUP

Scenario

You have completed these steps:

1. Determined how RIS works.

2. Investigated what changes and supporting infrastructure are necessary for RIS in your environment.

3. Determined server and client requirements both to support RIS and to implement RIS.

It is now time to begin the process of installing and configuring RIS prior to using it. You will need to explore some of the basic functionality of RIS so that you understand what RIS is doing as it installs itself.

Objectives

The goal of this lab is to begin the process of installing RIS in order to complete the lab. In a real-world setting, you should follow the installation of RIS with a reapplication of the latest Service Pack for Windows 2000 to guarantee that all operating system files are the current versions. If the RIS server is providing services for clients, such as File and Print or Domain Controller, be sure to either warn your clients that the server will be restarted or choose your installation for off-hours when the users will not be present. After completing this lab, you will be able to:

➤ Perform an installation of RIS on a server.

➤ Perform post-installation tasks on the server.

➤ Notify users that your server will be going off line temporarily.

Materials Required

This lab will require the following:

➤ Access to *Windows 2000 Server Resource Kit, Supplement 1*

➤ Access to a Windows 2000 Server with AD installed

➤ Access to the Windows 2000 Server installation media

➤ Access to the Windows 2000 Professional installation media

➤ Current Windows 2000 Service Pack

Activity Prerequisites

Lab is to be set up as stated in the Lab Setup Guide.

ACTIVITY

You are now ready to install and configure RIS. You will need a server running Windows 2000 Server (not necessarily AD) and access to the Windows 2000 installation media. Once you have these, you are ready to begin the process.

13

1. On the Windows 2000 Server, click **Start**, point to **Settings**, point to **Control Panel**, and click **Add/Remove Programs**. Then click **Add/Remove Windows Components**, scroll down the list, and choose **Remote Installation Services**. You should see the view shown in Figure 13-1.

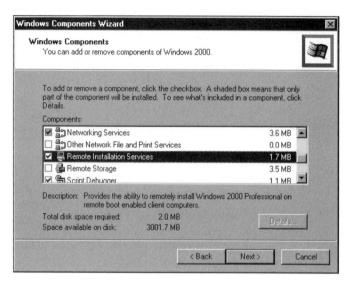

Figure 13-1   The selection box for installling RIS on a Windows 2000 server

2. Click this option and then click **Next**. You may see the Insert Disk dialog box shown in Figure 13-2. If so, provide either the installation media or the local path to the requested file.

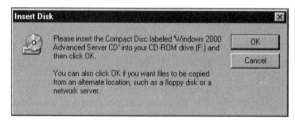

Figure 13-2   You will probably be prompted with this dialog looking for media

3. Click **OK** to proceed. The required file is named **risetup.ex_**, as shown in Figure 13-3. Once you locate this file, highlight it and then click **Open**.

Figure 13-3   The name and location of the RIS setup file from the installation media

4. You should see the **Configuring Components** progress screen next. See Figure 13-4. Allow the configuration to continue to the end.

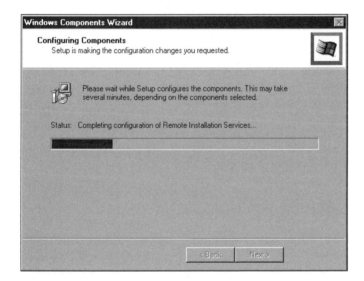

Figure 13-4   The reconfiguration progress bar; it may take several minutes to complete

5. When the process completes, click **Finish**, and you will see the screen shown in Figure 13-5. If you have access to the latest Windows 2000 Service Pack, click **No** and then install your Service Pack before allowing the computer to reboot. If you do not have access to the Service Pack, then allow the machine to reboot and remember that, in the real world, the preferred approach would be to install the Service Pack at this point.

Figure 13-5 The dialog asking your permission for the restart

6. When your Server reboots, you will need to configure your RIS Service. Clic[k] **Start**, point to **Settings**, point to **Control Panel**, and click **Add/Remove Programs**. Then click Add/Remove Windows Components and click the **Configure** button for RIS, as shown in Figure 13-6.

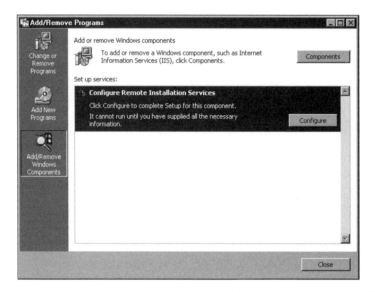

Figure 13-6   This view indicates that RIS has not yet been configured; it will not be seen after the configuration tool finishes

7. This is a Wizard-based tool. To move through the Wizard, click **Next** or supply the requested parameters and click **Next**.

8. The first screen you will encounter is titled Remote Installation Folder Location and is the location for the installation folder structure. The requirements for this selection are:

   a. A partition formatted with NTFS

   b. Enough free space to hold installation files

   c. The first NTFS partition that contains the boot.ini file and is not the boot volume (This is automatically selected.)

   d. A new directory named RemoteInstall (This is created at the root of this partition.)

9. Click **Next**.

10. You are next prompted to select the server's initial response to clients requesting RIS services. (See Figure 13-7.) For security reasons, be sure to leave this box unselected and click **Next**.

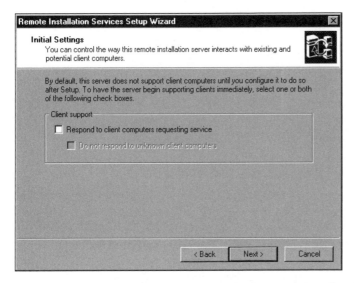

Figure 13-7   A security setting in RIS; be sure to leave the check box empty

11. You then need to provide the path to the Installation Source Files for Windows 2000 Professional. This will be a CD, a network, or a local install point. Be sure to point to a valid install point or you will not be allowed to proceed further. Click **Next**.

12. The next screen is titled Windows Installation Image Folder Name. Enter the name that you wish to use for this installation point and then click **Next**.

13. You will see a screen entitled Friendly Description and Help Text. The name of this screen is exactly descriptive of its function. Provide the required information and click **Next**.

14. At the conclusion of the wizard, you will see the screen shown in Figure 13-8, which will allow you to confirm your configuration settings. Click **Finish** to close the wizard.

13

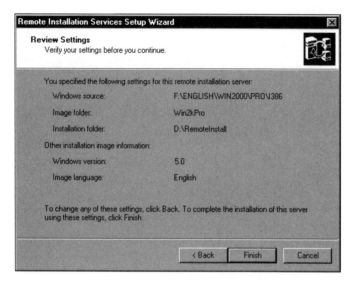

Figure 13-8   Your chance to review RIS settings one more time

15. The wizard will now begin copying files to be used in the RIS process. There are nine steps to complete in the process, as shown in Figure 13-9.

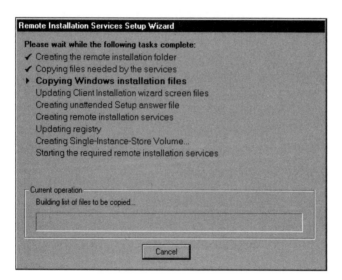

Figure 13-9   The RIS configuration wizard progress screen

16. When the process is complete, click the **Finish** button. You have now installed and configured RIS using the RISetup utility.

AB **13.5** CREATING **RIS** IMAGES

Lab Scenario

You have now installed your RIS server and configured the server to provide RIS services. Next, you need to provide images for the RIS process. You will need to make some decisions about the kind of images you want to provide. Do you want to provide a true unattended installation or do you want to provide a RIPrep image?

Objectives

The goal of this lab is to configure your RIS images. One method consists of using the Windows 2000 Setup Manager Wizard, which is available with the Windows 2000 Server Resource Kit. This is a Wizard-based tool that walks you through the process of creating an unattended setup file for use with the RIS process. You could also use the RIPREP tool that installs with RIS. This tool creates an image based upon a preconfigured "model" machine that has been built and preconfigured. You need to determine which approach is a better solution for your environment. After completing this lab, you will be able to:

> ➤ Use Setup Manager to build setup files.

> ➤ Use RIPrep to create images.

> ➤ Understand the differences in each tool.

> ➤ Understand the advantages in each tool.

Materials Required

This lab will require the following:

> ➤ Access to *Windows 2000 Server Resource Kit, Supplement 1*

> ➤ Access to a Windows 2000 Server with AD installed

> ➤ Access to the Windows 2000 Server installation media

> ➤ Current Windows 2000 Service Pack

Activity Prerequisites

Lab is to be set up as stated in the Lab Setup Guide.

ACTIVITY

This is a hands-on planning lab. Work as a team to fully explore these two techniques. If you have not already done so, install the Windows 2000 Server Resource Kit on your server. Then access the Server Resource Kit using the path shown in Figure 13-10.

13

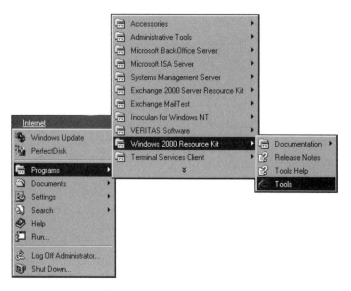

Figure 13-10   The path to the Windows 2000 Server Resource Kit tools

Choose the folder named Alphabetical List of Tools and then look for the tool named Setup Manager (Setupmgr.exe). Open this tool and begin the process of creating an unattended setup file. See Figure 13-11 for a view of the opening page of this tool.

Figure 13-11   The Windows 2000 Setup Manager wizard

Explore the tool completely to understand the options that are available to you.

The RIPrep is more complicated. This tool requires that you build a model machine configured as all client machines should be configured. The RIPrep tool is then used to capture an image of the hard drives, which can be deployed to many different machines. If you have an extra machine available, experiment with this tool also.

Make certain that you understand the differences between an unattended installation process and a disk image process. After you have completed your exploration of the tools, discuss with your team members the role that each tool could play in a corporate environment.

AB 13.6 CREATING AND TROUBLESHOOTING RIS BOOT DISKS

Lab Scenario

You are trying to use the RIS process to build new computers for your users; however, you just discovered that none of their NIC cards support the PXE standard. You need to make a RIS Boot Floppy Disk as a workaround for this. This short lab walks you through the process.

Objectives

Your goal in this lab is to create a RIS Boot Floppy Disk for starting a computer remotely and connecting to a RIS server. After completing this lab, you will be able to:

➤ Create a RIS Boot Floppy Disk.

Materials Required

This lab will require the following:

➤ Access to *Windows 2000 Server Resource Kit, Supplement 1*

➤ Access to a Windows 2000 Server with AD installed

➤ Access to the Windows 2000 Server installation media

➤ Current Windows 2000 Service Pack

➤ One blank 3.5" floppy disk

13

Activity Prerequisites

Lab is to be set up as stated in the Lab Setup Guide.

ACTIVITY

You need to create the RIS Boot Floppy disk. The process is simple.

1. Insert a 3.5" floppy disk. The disk does not need to be blank, since the tool will erase the disk before it copies files. Click **Start** and click **Run**. Type the following command line:
\\RIS_SERVER\RemoteInstall\admin\i386\rbfg.exe and click **OK**.

2. You will see the screen shown in Figure 13-12.

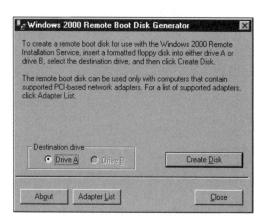

Figure 13-12 The RIS boot floppy disk setup screen

3. Click **Create Disk**. When the process is complete, you will see the screen shown in Figure 13-13.

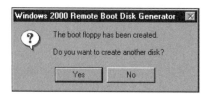

Figure 13-13 If you need to create more RIS floppies, click Yes

4. You have finished the process.

LAB 13.7 MANAGING RIS SECURITY

Lab Scenario

You and your design team need to implement RIS Security settings in your corporate environment to control who can and who cannot download the RIS images. How can you implement this? Your task in this lab will be to investigate this process.

Objectives

The goal of this lab is to use a variety of methods to restrict access to RIS images stored on your RIS server. Several different techniques are available, including NTFS permissions, shared folder permissions, GPO configuration, and prestaging the RIS accounts. It will be up to you and your design team to arrive at the best solution for your environment. What might be correct for your team may not be what another team would choose. Assign roles and responsibilities to each team member. Have each member report back to the team with their findings. Be prepared to explain your choices when you present in front of the class. After completing this lab, you will be able to:

➤ Implement RIS Security.

➤ Assign appropriate NTFS and shared folder permissions to RIS resources.

➤ Understand how to pre-stage a RIS account in AD.

➤ Configure AD GPOs to support RIS.

Materials Required

This lab will require the following:

➤ Access to *Windows 2000 Server Resource Kit, Supplement 1*

➤ Access to a Windows 2000 Server with AD installed

Activity Prerequisites

Lab is to be set up as stated in the Lab Setup Guide.

ACTIVITY

Assemble your design team and create a design for an AD RIS server security implementation. Your design goal is that only authorized users can access the RIS server and download an image, and then only when you have enabled their account for such a download. Compare your findings and results with other team members in the class and be prepared to explain your decisions.

13

LAB **13.8** TROUBLESHOOTING THE **RIS** PROCESS

Lab Scenario

Several things can go wrong with RIS. They range from very simple things within your control to some complex things beyond your control.

Objectives

Your goal in this lab is to create a list of things that can go wrong with RIS. These problems could involve hardware issues, configuration issues, AD issues, and security issues. If you decide to implement RIS in your environment, such knowledge would be very useful. After completing this lab, you will be able to:

➤ Troubleshoot RIS.

➤ Troubleshoot AD and RIS.

➤ Apply corrective actions for faulty RIS functionality.

➤ Diagnose RIS problems.

Materials Required

This lab will require the following:

➤ Access to *Windows 2000 Server Resource Kit, Supplement 1*

➤ Access to a Windows 2000 Server with AD installed

Activity Prerequisites

Lab is to be set up as stated in the Lab Setup Guide.

ACTIVITY

As preparation, consider the following questions. Are there any issues with RIS server and AD configurations? Your clients have the correct version of PXE on their NIC card but are unable to reach the RIS server. What should you check? Your clients have NIC cards that do not support PXE. Can you provide any help for them? Your NIC cards are not on the list included with the RIS Boot Floppies. What can you do?

Create a document that provides your design team with troubleshooting solutions for RIS. Investigate possible problems and solutions in the Server Resource Kit. Work with your team members to arrive at useful solutions for the different problems that can affect RIS services and functionalities. Present your findings to other teams in class and be prepared to explain them.

CHAPTER FOURTEEN

ACTIVE DIRECTORY REPLICATION

Labs included in this chapter

➤ Lab 14.1 Active Directory Replication

➤ Lab 14.2 Configuring and Using REPLMON and REPADMIN

➤ Lab 14.3 Active Directory Replication Illustrated

➤ Lab 14.4 Intra-site Replication

➤ Lab 14.5 Inter-site Replication

➤ Lab 14.6 Site-link Bridges and Replication

➤ Lab 14.7 Monitoring Replication

➤ Lab 14.8 Fine-Tuning the Replication Process

Microsoft MCSE Exam #70-217 Objectives	
Objective	Lab
Managing, Monitoring, and Optimizing the Components of Active Directory	14.1, 14.2, 14.3, 14.4, 14.5, 14.6, 14.7, 14.8
Configuring, Managing, Monitoring, and Troubleshooting Security in a Directory Services Infrastructure	14.7, 14.8

LAB 14.1 ACTIVE DIRECTORY REPLICATION

Lab Scenario

Your design team, through hard work and perseverance, has created a usable, function: Active Directory implementation. Your corporate infrastructure consists of two domair that support Thisbin Co. and Kronk Designs, respectively. These two domains have fou domain controllers, two in each domain. The structure of the two domains is:

➤ **Thisbin.com**

- Thisbin1_DC

- Thisbin2_DC

➤ **Kronk.biz**

- Kronk1_DC

- Kronk2_DC

Your network consists of two separate sites that constitute two physical buildings sepa- rated by approximately 100 miles. The two networks are connected by satellite uplink Together they exist in one AD Forest and have two Global Catalog servers, Thisbin1 anc Kronk2. One GC is located in each domain. See Figures 14-1 and 14-2.

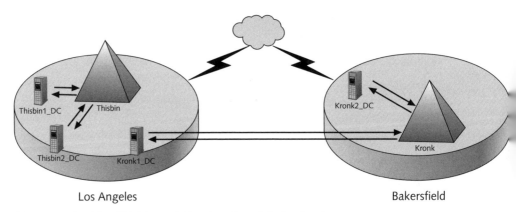

Los Angeles   Bakersfield

Figure 14-1   The Thisbin and Kronk network infrastructure

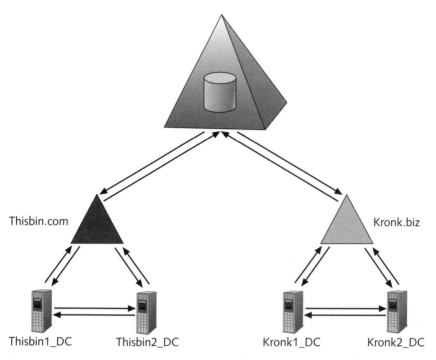

Thisbin.com

Kronk.biz

Thisbin1_DC   Thisbin2_DC   Kronk1_DC   Kronk2_DC

Figure 14-2   A view of the AD Forest for Thisbin Co. and Kronk Designs

You may need to reference these figures for the remainder of this Chapter.

Objectives

Based on the diagrams above, you will answer some basic questions concerning Active Directory Replication. You may need to use the *Windows 2000 Server Resource Kit, Supplement 1* or the online Help in Windows 2000. Work with a lab partner to answer the questions. After completing this lab, you will be able to:

➤ Identify the components of Active Directory Replication.

➤ Identify the technologies used for replication.

➤ Identify replication topologies.

Materials Required

This lab will require the following:

➤ Access to *Windows 2000 Server Resource Kit, Supplement 1*

➤ Access to a Windows 2000 Server with Active Directory installed

Activity Prerequisites

Lab is to be set up as stated in the Lab Setup Guide.

ACTIVITY

Using Figure 14-1 and Figure 14-2 as references, answer the questions below. You may nee~~~ the *Windows 2000 Server Resource Kit, Supplement 1.* The *Windows Online Help* manual ma~~~ also be useful.

1. What replication technology is being used between Los Angeles and Bakersfield?

2. What replication technology is being used to replicate data between Thisbin1_DC and Thisbin2_DC?

3. What replication technology do the servers Kronk1_DC and Kronk2_DC use for replication? Is this the same technology used by Thisbin1_DC and Thisbin2_DC?

4. Can Thisbin1_DC and Thisbin2_DC be forced to use the same technology as Kronk1_DC and Kronk2_DC if the latter two servers are replicating with SMTP?

5. Why or why not?

6. What replication technologies can be used in the Kronk domain between the domain controllers?

7. What is the replication control technology for the Thisbin domain? What service is responsible for managing the replication in that environment? Where does this service run?

LAB 14.2 CONFIGURING AND USING REPLMON AND REPADMIN

Lab Scenario

If you are planning to monitor AD Replication or if you are planning to exercise any form of control over AD Replication, you must have access to the appropriate AD tools. The tools in question are REPLMON and REPADMIN. Neither tool is installed as part of the normal installation of Windows 2000 Server. Both tools must be installed after the fact. They also install with additional tools over and above those that are provided with the Windows 2000 Server Resource Kit. These optional tools together are called the Windows 2000 Support Tools. The tools included are:

➤ Active Directory Administration Tool

➤ Active Directory Replication Monitor

➤ ADSI Edit

➤ Application Compatibility Tool

➤ Command Prompt

➤ Dependency Walker

➤ Disk Probe

Do not use Disk Probe until you have read the documentation for it. Misuse of this tool can permanently destroy all data on your hard drive.

➤ Global Flags Editor

➤ Process Viewer

➤ Security Administration Tools

➤ SNMP Query Utility (Simple Network Management Protocol)

➤ Windiff

See Figure 14-3.

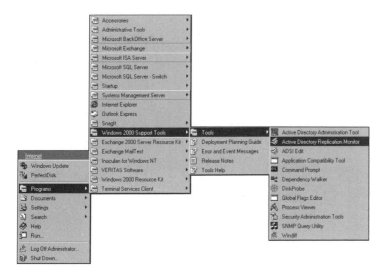

Figure 14-3   Opening REPLMON

Notice that REPADMIN is not listed in this tool set since it is a command line tool. In total, there are 43 separate tools that install as part of this tool set. Only a few of the tools are GUI-based. Most can be useful for the day-to-day administration of Windows 2000 Active Directory.

Objectives

The goal of this lab is to install the Windows 2000 Support Tools and learn some of the basic functionality of both REPLMON and REPADMIN. You may also experiment and discover the functionality of the remaining tools, although they will not be discussed in this lab. After completing this lab, you will be able to:

➤ Install the Windows 2000 Support Tools.

➤ Access, perform preliminary configuration of, and use REPLMON.

➤ Access and use REPADMIN.

Materials Required

This lab will require the following:

➤ Access to *Windows 2000 Server Resource Kit, Supplement 1*

➤ Access to a Windows 2000 Server with Active Directory installed

➤ Access to the Windows 2000 Server Installation Media

Activity Prerequisites

Lab is to be set up as stated in the Lab Setup Guide.

ACTIVITY

You will install the tools using the following procedure.

1. Insert the installation media and navigate to the path **Support | Tools | Setup.exe**.

2. Run the **Setup.exe** file, which will produce the screen shown in Figure 14-4.

Figure 14-4 The initial installation screen for the Support Tools

3. Click **Next** to continue. Enter your name and organization information and click **Next**.

4. Click the **Typical** radio button for the installation and then click **Next**. See Figure 14-5.

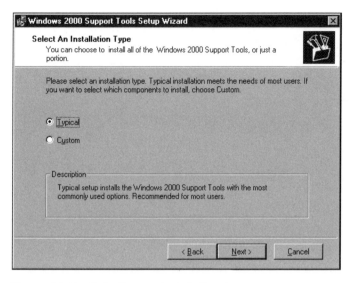

Figure 14-5   Selecting an installation type

5. Click **Next** a second time to begin the installation. See Figure 14-6.

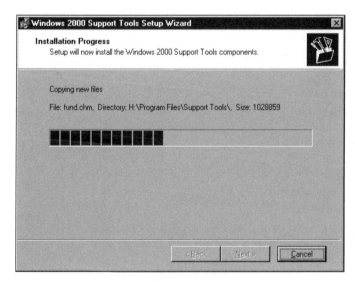

Figure 14-6   The installation progress bar

6. Click **Finish** to end the installation. It is not necessary to reboot to complete the installation. The tools are ready for use immediately. See Figure 14-7.

14

Figure 14-7   Completing the Installation Wizard

7. You may now open REPLMON. Click **Start**, point to **Programs**, point to **Windows 2000 Support Tools**, point to **Tools**, and click **Active Directory Replication Monitor**. Then double-click **Active Directory Replication Monitor**. You will now see the view of the tool shown in Figure 14–8.

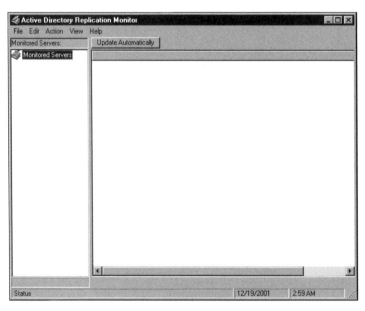

Figure 14-8   The opening screen for REPLMON

8. The tool does not populate itself by default so you must populate it. To do this, right-click the **Monitored Servers** button and choose the option **Add Monitored Server**. See Figure 14-9.

Figure 14-9   Adding a Monitored Server to REPLMON

9. On the next screen for this version of the tool, you must select the option **Search the directory for the server to add**. This entry should self-populate with the name of the parent domain, as shown in Figure 14-10.

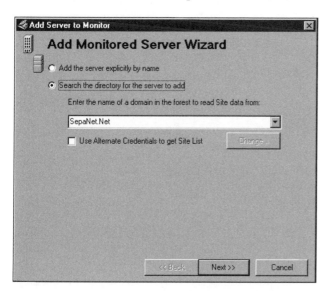

Figure 14-10   The Add Monitored Server Wizard

10. Click **Next** to proceed. You may then either click the first radio button with a label beginning with **Below is a list of Sites**..., then expand **Default-First-Site-Name** and choose your server, or you may click the radio button with a label beginning with **Enter the name**..., and then type the name of the server to monitor. This approach is shown in Figure 14-11.

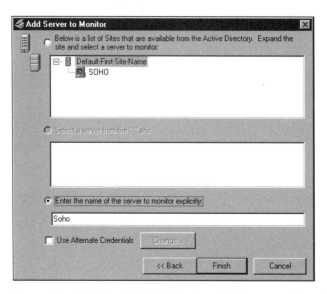

Figure 14-11 Viewing the list of available servers to add to REPLMON

11. Click **Finish**. It may take a few minutes to populate the information.

12. You will now see a view that looks like Figure 14-12.

13. This view shows the three partitions contained within AD: the Schema partition, the Configuration partition, and the Domain partition. What are these partitions for?

14. If you have child domains, you will see additional domains listed below your own domain information. You will only see one entry each for Schema and Configuration, however. If you right-click the domain controller, you will see this menu and listing of available functions, as shown in Figure 14-13.

Figure 14-12   REPLMON is populated and listing the replicated AD partitions

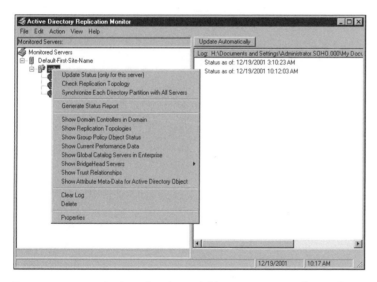

Figure 14-13   The list of tools available in REPLMON for working with your domain controllers

15. Many of these tools are extremely useful and you are encouraged to explore them further; however, now click **Synchronize Each Directory Partition with All Servers**. This will open the screen shown in Figure 14-14.

16. Select the appropriate option and click **OK**. You will be asked if you are certain that you want to initiate this action. Click **Yes** to proceed.

17. Allow approximately five minutes for the replication to occur and then refresh the view of REPLMON to confirm replication.

14

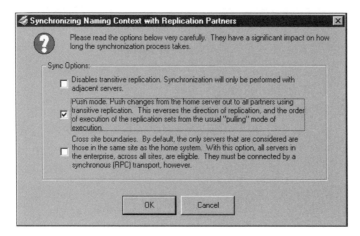

Figure 14-14   Configuring replication options for the replicated partitions

      18. The REPADMIN tool requires no configuration beyond its installation. The use of this tool is left as an exercise for the students. However, careless use of this tool can damage your Active Directory implementation. Review the use of this tool in the Server Resource Kit and also in the on-line Help tool in Windows 2000. You will need to use the Windows 2000 Support Tools Help in order to complete this section of the lab. You will be expected to have working knowledge of the REPADMIN tool if you are planning to partici-pate in the Microsoft Windows 2000 MCSE certification process.

LAB 14.3 ACTIVE DIRECTORY REPLICATION ILLUSTRATED

Lab Scenario

Shown below is an illustration of an Active Directory implementation. It is the same illus-tration that appeared earlier in the chapter.

You will now examine the workings of Active Directory as a lab exercise.

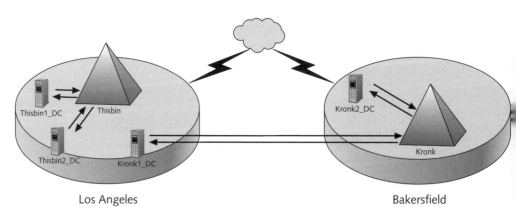

Objectives

The goal for this lab is to more fully understand the workings of Active Directory replication using a paper-based model. After completing this lab, you will be able to:

➤ Understand the difference between Inter-site replication and Intra-site replication.

➤ Understand Global Catalog replication.

➤ Understand replication across a WAN link.

Materials Required

This lab will require the following:

➤ Access to *Windows 2000 Server Resource Kit, Supplement 1*

➤ Access to a Windows 2000 Server with Active Directory installed

➤ Access to the Windows 2000 Server Installation Media

➤ Answers from Lab 14.1

Activity Prerequisites

Lab is to be set up as stated in the Lab Setup Guide.

ACTIVITY

Using Figure 14-1, answer the following questions.

1. What three Active Directory partitions are present in this diagram that are shared between the Thisbin domain and the Kronk domain?

2. What technology is used to replicate between the Thisbin domain controllers?

3. What technology is used to replicate between the Kronk domain controllers?

4. Is the fact that the Thisbin domain controllers exist entirely within a LAN environment versus the mixed LAN/WAN environment of the Kronk domain significant in terms of AD replication? Why?

5. What replication technology that might be implemented for the Kronk domain cannot be implemented for the Thisbin domain?

6. A user's telephone number is changed in AD on Thisbin2_DC. Diagram the replication path from Thisbin2_DC to Kronk1_DC.

7. In Question 6 above, what is the default replication latency from Thisbin2_DC to Thisbin1_DC?

8. What is the default replication latency from Kronk2_DC to Kronk1_DC?

14

LAB 14.4 INTRA-SITE REPLICATION

Lab Scenario

There is are many aspects to Intra-site replication, such as the mechanics of Intra-site replication, the possible configuration options available, and the frequency with which Intra-site replication occurs.

Objectives

The goal of this lab will be to research AD Intra-site replication and then answer several questions to test your knowledge of the concepts. After completing this lab, you will be able to:

➤ Understand the implementation of AD Intra-site replication.

➤ Understand the operation of the KCC.

➤ Know how to manually configure the KCC.

➤ Understand the KCC replication mapping topology.

Materials Required

This lab will require the following:

➤ Access to *Windows 2000 Server Resource Kit, Supplement 1*

➤ Access to a Windows 2000 Server with Active Directory installed

Activity Prerequisites

Lab is to be set up as stated in the Lab Setup Guide.

ACTIVITY

You will investigate the behavior of AD Intra-site replication during this lab.

1. Describe the steps necessary to install AD Intra-site replication.

2. Following is a diagram showing four domain controllers in a single domain. Draw the replication paths implemented in this environment. (See Figure 14-15.)

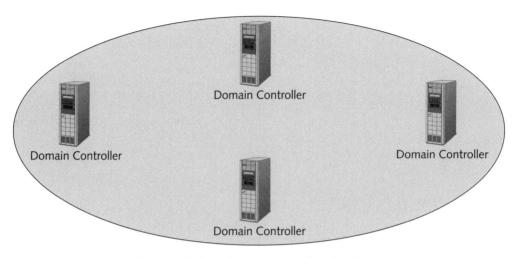

Figure 14-15   A simple site with four domain controllers for determining KCC operation

3. Below is a diagram showing nine domain controllers in a single domain. Draw the replication paths implemented for this domain. (See Figure 14-16.)

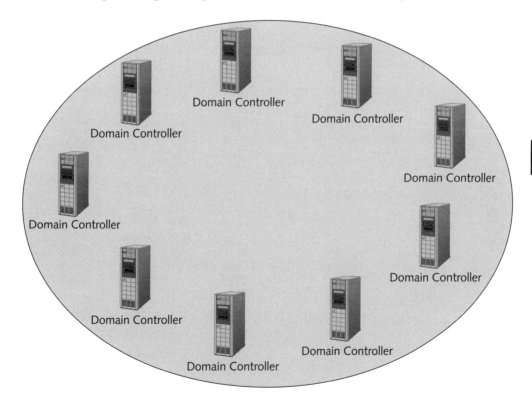

Figure 14-16   A more complicated view to demonstrate KCC functionality

14

4. In order to achieve reduced replication latency in your environment, you need to modify the replication frequency for the KCC. How is this done?

5. Returning to Figure 14-16, if one of the domain controllers in the diagram fails, how will the KCC react?

6. You have had a significant event in your environment. It is necessary to readjust the replication topology before the next automatic synchronization. You do not want to initiate replication. How can you synchronize the replication topology without causing replication?

LAB 14.5 INTER-SITE REPLICATION

Lab Scenario

There are many aspects to Inter-site replication, such as the mechanics of Inter-site replication, the possible configuration options available, and the frequency with which Inter-site replication occurs.

Objectives

The goal for this lab is to discover AD Inter-site replication and then answer several questions to test your knowledge of the concepts. After completing this lab, you should be able to:

➤ Understand the implementation of AD Inter-site replication.

➤ Understand the operation of the ISTG.

➤ Know how to manually configure the ISTG.

➤ Understand the ISTG replication mapping topology.

Materials Required

This lab will require the following:

➤ Access to *Windows 2000 Server Resource Kit, Supplement 1*

➤ Access to a Windows 2000 Server with Active Directory installed

Activity Prerequisites

Lab is to be set up as stated in the Lab Setup Guide.

ACTIVITY

You will investigate the behavior of AD Inter-site replication during this lab.

1. When dealing with Inter-site replication, manual configuration of the connectivity is required. What is the difference between a **site** and a **site-link**?

2. What is the default replication interval, in minutes, for Inter-site replication?

3. Complete the table below detailing the differences between Intra-site replication and Inter-site replication.

Intra-site replication	Inter-site replication

4. Is Inter-site replication an automatic service or a scheduled service?

5. Describe the steps necessary to configure Inter-site replication.

6. Below is a diagram illustrating a situation in your environment. There are three sites involved in the process: **Detroit**, **Tokyo**, and **London**. All times shown are local.

Site Name	Scheduled Replication	Window Opens	Window Closes	Replication Frequency
Detroit	Y	8:30	16:30	0:45
Tokyo	Y	8:30	16:30	0:45
London	Y	8:30	16:30	0:45

Also, refer to the diagram shown in Figure 14-17.

All three sites are experiencing replication problems. London can achieve only partial replication with Detroit and Tokyo. Detroit can achieve only partial replication with London and no replication with Tokyo. Tokyo can achieve only partial replication with London and no replication with Detroit. Troubleshoot the problem and record your conclusions.

14

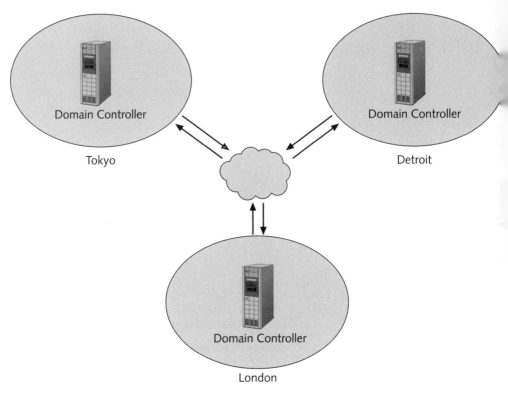

Figure 14-17   An Inter-site replication problem

LAB 14.6 SITE-LINK BRIDGES AND REPLICATION

Lab Scenario

Inter-site replication is replication that occurs between two sites in Active Directory. A
such, as you learned in the previous lab, it requires configuration. This lab deals with some
of those configuration issues.

Objectives

The goal of this lab is to explore the issues involving the configuration of Site-link
Bridges. You will investigate the conditions under which they should be used and how to
use them. After completing this lab, you will be able to:

> ➤ Recognize what a Site-link Bridge is.

> ➤ Recognize when to use a Site-link Bridge.

> ➤ Recognize why you should use a Site-link Bridge.

> ➤ Recognize Site-link Bridge configuration issues.

Materials Required

This lab will require the following:

➤ Access to *Windows 2000 Server Resource Kit, Supplement 1*

➤ Access to a Windows 2000 Server with Active Directory installed

Activity Prerequisites

Lab is to be set up as stated in the Lab Setup Guide.

ACTIVITY

During the course of this lab, you will investigate the use and application of Site-link Bridges.

    1. Refer to Figure 14-18.

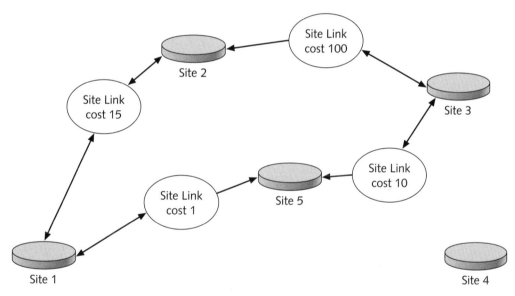

Figure 14-18   A Site-link connection problem

14

Some facts about this diagram:

This is a partially routed environment. Site 1 is reachable through routers from Site 2 and Site 5. Site 2 is reachable through routers from Site 1 and Site 3. Site 3 is reachable through routers from Site 2 and Site 5. Site 5 is reachable through routers from Site 1 and Site 3. Site 4 is unreachable from any site. Troubleshoot this environment. What should be configured?

    2. Using the same diagram, what is the Site-link cost from Site 1 to Site 3 using the preferred route?

    3. What is Microsoft's suggested setting for a standard route cost?

4. What does the Site-link cost represent?

5. Examine Figure 14-19. What do DCs 1, 2, and 4 represent and how do they work?

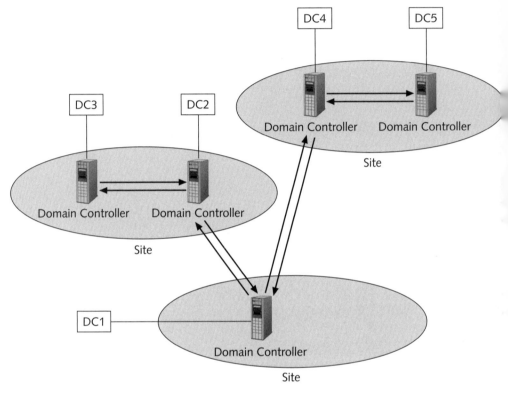

Figure 14-19 The concept of Bridgehead Servers illustrated

LAB **14.7** MONITORING REPLICATION

Lab Scenario

As part of your AD replication configuration, you need to monitor replication. What tools are available to you? Are there tools readily available to you?

Objectives

The goal for this lab is to experiment with tools that will allow you to monitor Active Directory. After completing this lab, you will be able to use the following tools:

➤ Event Viewer

➤ REPLMON

➤ REPADMIN

➤ LDP.exe

➤ Netdiag

➤ Netsh

Materials Required

This lab will require the following:

➤ Access to *Windows 2000 Server Resource Kit, Supplement 1*

➤ Access to a Windows 2000 Server with Active Directory installed

Activity Prerequisites

Lab is to be set up as stated in the Lab Setup Guide.

ACTIVITY

As your activity for this lab, explore the use of the tools listed above. You will find that they can be extremely useful, particularly the command-line tools, in troubleshooting and monitoring AD. Work in groups to discover the complete functionality of the tools. Be sure to trigger replication in your domain environment in order to use the tools.

LAB 14.8 FINE-TUNING THE REPLICATION PROCESS

Lab Scenario

Your corporate environment exists as several separate sites. Some sites are supported by routers and others are not. You have the KCC on your internal replication links running with its default settings. You have also left your ISTG settings on their default values. As a result, you are experiencing replication latency issues, particularly site-to-site. There are several other issues that need to be addressed.

14

Objectives

The goal of this lab is to perform the following actions in your AD environment to affect the performance of AD Replication. After completing this lab, you will be able to:

➤ Adjust the replication latency for Intra-Site replication.

➤ Force replication from the command line.

➤ Adjust the replication latency for Inter-site replication.

➤ Design AD replication to fully support a corporate environment distributed across several different time zones.

➤ Enable AD logging.

➤ Use the Event Viewer to monitor AD.

Materials Required

This lab will require the following:

➤ Access to *Windows 2000 Server Resource Kit, Supplement 1*

➤ Access to a Windows 2000 Server with Active Directory installed

Activity Prerequisites

Lab is to be set up as stated in the Lab Setup Guide.

ACTIVITY

This is a planning lab. Assemble your design team and begin the process of modifyin AD replication. Remember that any modification of Active Directory should always b done as a group project so as to minimize any negative impact on the AD structure. AI to you is a database to manage. To your employer or corporate customer, it is their entir world. Take a tip from carpenters—"*Measure twice, cut once.*" The same underlying con cept should be applied in AD. Be sure that you understand the implications of what yo are doing before you implement the new or revised functionality. Make certain that al members of your design team have roles assigned to them. Prepare your documents an be prepared to present your decisions/findings to the entire class following the lab. B prepared to justify your decisions and findings. Be sure to fully utilize the available ref erence material.

SECURITY

Microsoft MCSE Exam #70-217 Objectives	
Objective	**Lab**
Configuring, Managing, Monitoring, Optimizing, and Troubleshooting Change and Configuration Management	15.8, 15.9
Managing, Monitoring, and Optimizing the Components of Active Directory	15.2, 15.5
Configuring, Managing, Monitoring, and Troubleshooting Security in a Directory Services Infrastructure	15.1, 15.2, 15.3, 15.4, 15.5, 15.7, 15.8, 15.9

LAB 15.1 AUDITING CONCEPTS

Lab Scenario

Your AD implementation has been up and running for a few months now and you a▪
pleased with the results. However, management has approached you with a new concer▪
They would like to know if it is possible to track security and resource access in the fore▪

Objectives

The goal of this first lab is to understand some of the basic concepts of the application ▪
auditing in Windows 2000. These include what can and cannot be audited, as well ▪
whether there are setup issues associated with auditing. After completing this lab, you wi▪
be able to:

➤ Understand basic auditing concepts.

➤ Understand what file formats support auditing.

➤ Understand the importance of planning an audit policy.

Materials Required

This lab will require the following:

➤ Access to *Windows 2000 Server Resource Kit, Supplement 1*

➤ Access to a Windows 2000 Server with Active Directory installed

Activity Prerequisites

Lab is to be set up as stated in the Lab Setup Guide.

ACTIVITY

Divide into design teams and begin the process of exploring auditing in Windows 2000▪
After you have explored some concepts, answer the questions below.

1. What file systems support auditing?

2. What is the procedure for implementing auditing on a Windows 98 client?

3. One of the constraints management has placed upon you is the necessity to audit how frequently specific applications are being used and who is using them. Is this possible?

4. Can auditing be enabled for operating system-specific functions?

5. Where can auditing information be viewed?

6. Who can configure auditing?

7. Who can view the information collected by auditing?

LAB 15.2 PLANNING YOUR AUDIT POLICY—LOCAL AND DOMAIN AUDITS

Lab Scenario

Now that you have explored general auditing concepts, it is time to apply these concepts. Your company would like a fully implemented auditing plan for your AD forest. You will need to take into account users and computers. Not all of your users belong to the domain; some have only local accounts (no domain account). Additionally, you need to implement auditing on your print devices, including FAX machines, and your servers, both domain controllers and file/print servers.

Objectives

The goal of this lab is to work with your design team and plan your AD audit policy. Use the guidelines to arrive at your policy. You will need to design an audit policy that fully supports the requirements stated and yet is not so cumbersome as to be oppressive to manage or implement. After completing this lab, you will be able to:

➤ Design an efficient audit policy.

➤ Make design decisions and tradeoffs where required, trading performance for manageability while collecting the required level of information.

➤ Arrive at a plan to collect and review the returned audit information.

Materials Required

This lab will require the following:

➤ Access to *Windows 2000 Server Resource Kit, Supplement 1*

➤ Access to a Windows 2000 Server with Active Directory installed

➤ An implementation of Windows 2000 Active Directory

Activity Prerequisites

Lab is to be set up as stated in the Lab Setup Guide.

ACTIVITY

Assemble a design team and assign specific roles to each individual. Be sure to select a team lead who will be responsible for coordinating all aspects of the design. The team will also make the presentation in front of the class. Formulate an effective audit policy based on the criteria given below and remember to design policies that will be effective both locally and at the domain. You will need to weigh and balance usefulness of the information versus security needs versus performance issues for your design. In other words, in order to collect particular information, consider whether you are imposing an unacceptable level of performance upon either the users as a group or the forest in general. Determine whether the information is valuable to the business. When you design your audit policy, be sure to include representatives from the business to provide input as to what material must ▮ included in the policy. What material would the business like to collect? Prepare your pl₂ now, but do not implement it yet. Present it to the class and accept constructive criticis concerning your implementation. The information that you will build your audit pl₂ around is given below.

Affected Object	Logon	Logoff	Access	System Access	Attempt to Change Password	Attempt to Change System Settings	Success	Failure	File and Object Access	Printer Access
Domain Users	X		X	X	X	X	X	X	X	X
Domain Guests	X							X		X
Admins	X	X	X	X	X	X		X		
Server Operators	X			X	X	X		X		
Everyone	X						X	X	X	
Print Users	X		X					X		X
IIS Users	X			X	X	X		X	X	

For this lab, you may not redesign your OU structure. You must use your current implementation.

Lab 15.3 Configuring Group Policy to Support Auditing

Lab Scenario

You have planned your audit policy for your local and domain users. It is now time to implement the support for auditing in Active Directory.

Objectives

The goal of this lab is to configure the domain to support AD auditing. You will learn the initial configuration steps necessary to activate auditing for your domain. After completing this lab, you will be able to:

➤ Configure auditing at the domain level in Active Directory.

➤ Learn the path in Active Directory Users and Computers to facilitate the domain implementation of auditing.

Materials Required

This lab will require the following:

➤ Access to *Windows 2000 Server Resource Kit, Supplement 1*

➤ Access to a Windows 2000 Server with Active Directory installed

Activity Prerequisites

Lab is to be set up as stated in the Lab Setup Guide.

ACTIVITY

You will use Active Directory Users and Computers to implement the support for auditing at the domain level. Follow the steps listed below.

1. Open Active Directory Users and Computers and then navigate to the following path: **Domain_name | Domain Controllers**. See Figure 15-1.

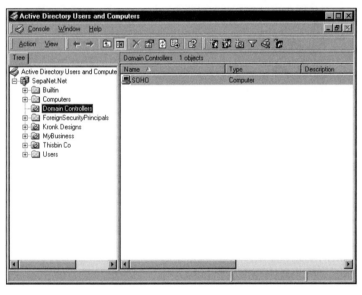

Figure 15-1   Active Directory Users and Computers opening view

2. Right-click the **Domain Controllers** OU and click **Properties**. Then click the **Group Policy** tab. See Figure 15-2.

15

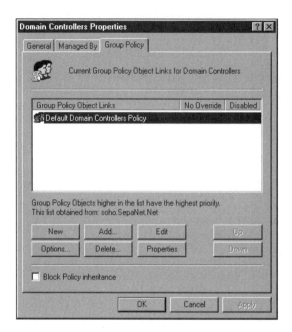

Figure 15-2   The Default Domain Controllers Group Policy Object

3. Click the **Edit** button. You want to edit the GPO named **Default Domain Controllers Policy**. You will now see the screen shown in Figure 15-3.

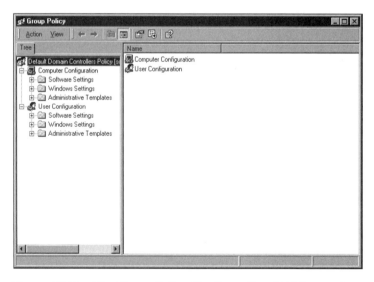

Figure 15-3   The Group Policy Configuration MMC snap-in

4. With this screen visible, expand the path **Computer Configuration | Windows Settings | Security Settings | Local Policies | Audit Policy**. See Figure 15-4.

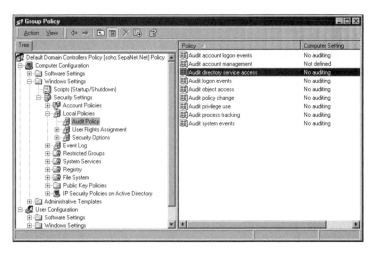

Figure 15-4   The initial auditing configuration for AD

5. Double-click the entry for **Audit directory service access** to bring up the screen shown in Figure 15-5.

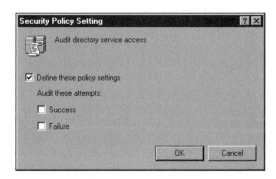

Figure 15-5   Use this screen to turn auditing on for the domain

6. Depending on the policy your group designed, choose the appropriate action—either **Success**, **Failure**, or both—and then click **OK**. See Figure 15-6.

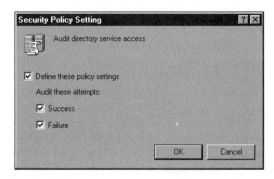

Figure 15-6   Auditing has now been enabled for the domain

15

7. It will take approximately five minutes for the GPO policy to become effective. At the end of five minutes, check the Active Directory Users and Computers tool on the other machine and you should see the newly created object in your partner's DC.

LAB 15.4 REQUIREMENTS FOR IMPLEMENTING AUDITING

Lab Scenario

Now that you have configured your domain to support auditing, you need to begin the process of implementing auditing for your domain.

Objectives

The goal of this lab is to determine who has the administrative rights and permissions to implement auditing for your domain at the domain level. You will also consider any other factors involved when implementing auditing for Windows 2000. After completing this lab, you will be able to:

➤ Determine who has permissions to implement auditing.

➤ Configure user accounts to grant those permissions.

Materials Required

This lab will require the following:

➤ Access to *Windows 2000 Server Resource Kit, Supplement 1*

➤ Access to a Windows 2000 Server with Active Directory installed

Activity Prerequisites

Lab is to be set up as stated in the Lab Setup Guide.

ACTIVITY

As a planning exercise, create a list of users in your domain, building on users who currently exist in the domain, who are to be granted permissions to:

➤ Configure auditing at the domain level.

➤ Configure auditing at the OU level.

➤ View audit logs.

➤ Archive audit logs.

Make sure that the list is comprehensive and provides for such eventualities as employees going on vacation or being out of the office for extended periods. You may grant one user several different permissions if necessary. Be prepared to justify your decisions.

AB 15.5 AUDITING FILES, FOLDERS, AND ACTIVE DIRECTORY OBJECTS

Lab Scenario

You will now configure auditing on resources in your domain. You will need to use your planning documents from Lab 15.2 to determine what and whom to audit.

Objectives

The goal of this lab is to apply an audit policy to your domain and selected files and folders. Since the process is essentially the same whether files, folders, or AD objects are being configured, only one object, file auditing, will be demonstrated in this lab. The application of folder auditing and AD object auditing is an exercise for the students. After completing this lab, you will be able to:

> Implement file object auditing.

> Implement folder object auditing.

> Implement AD object auditing.

Materials Required

This lab will require the following:

> Access to *Windows 2000 Server Resource Kit, Supplement 1*

> Access to a Windows 2000 Server with Active Directory installed

Activity Prerequisites

Lab is to be set up as stated in the Lab Setup Guide.

ACTIVITY

Follow the steps below to configure auditing for file objects. The steps for folders and AD objects are the same with additional steps required. These are left to the student to discover.

1. Select an NTFS partition on your computer and expand a folder to view individual files. You may use any GUI tool, including My Computer or Explorer. Use the view in Figure 15-7 as an example. Your view will be different.

2. Right-click an individual file and click **Properties**. See Figure 15-8.

15

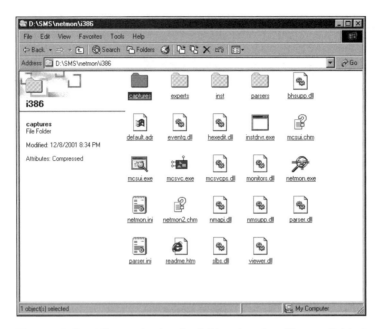

Figure 15-7   The contents of a folder showing files available for auditing

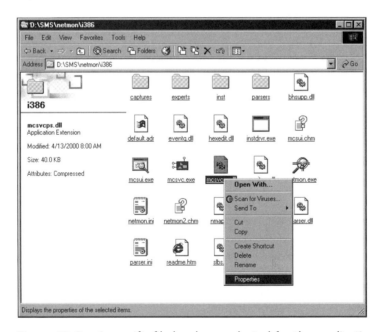

Figure 15-8   A specific file has been selected for the application of auditing

3. Click the **Security** tab and then click **Advanced**. Click the **Auditing** tab. Since this is the first time auditing has been configured, the Auditing Entries list should be empty. See Figure 15-9.

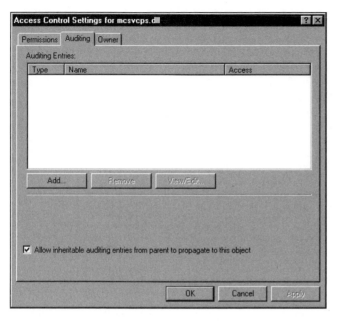

Figure 15-9   The empty list of audited objects

4. Click **Add** and select an account to add the Auditing Entries list. For this example, the Users group was chosen. When you click **OK**, the next screen is shown in Figure 15-10. This screen allows the configuration of the specific auditing options.

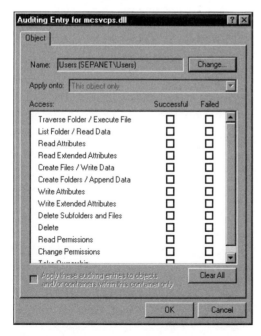

15

Figure 15-10   The list of auditing configuration options

5. Click the check boxes to choose auditing permissions as required by your audit policy, as shown in Figure 15-11.

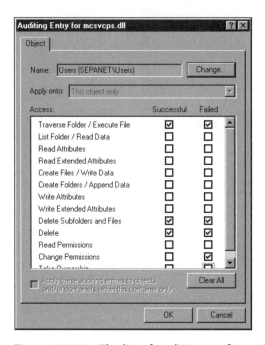

Figure 15-11   The list of auditing configuration options with several options selected

6. Click **OK** to accept the new settings and you will be returned to the screen shown in Figure 15-12. Note that the Auditing Entries list is now populated.

7. Decide whether you wish to allow inheritable permissions from the parent object to propagate to this object by clicking the check box for the appropriate setting, and then click **OK** twice.

8. You have now configured auditing on a file object. Proceed to configure the remaining required settings for your folder and AD objects.

9. When you have completed the configuration of auditing, examine the results by opening the Event Viewer tool and choosing the Security Log view. You should see audit information being collected, as shown in Figure 15-13.

You have completed the configuration and testing of an audit policy. Discuss whether you think your independent implementation worked.

Figure 15-12   A group of users have been selected for auditing, showing their access permissions

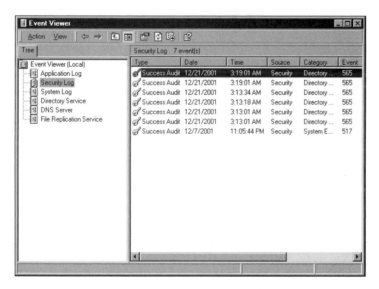

Figure 15-13   The Security Log view in Event Viewer showing auditing information being collected

15

Lab 15.6 Auditing Printers

Lab Scenario

You now need to configure auditing on your print devices. Determine appropriate leve of auditing and configure the settings as required.

Objectives

The goal for this lab is to determine an appropriate level of auditing for print devices i your domain and then apply those settings. After completing this lab, you will be able to

> ➤ Configure and apply auditing for print devices.

> ➤ Choose an appropriate level of auditing for those devices.

Materials Required

This lab will require the following:

> ➤ Access to *Windows 2000 Server Resource Kit, Supplement 1*

> ➤ Access to a Windows 2000 Server with Active Directory installed

Activity Prerequisites

Lab is to be set up as stated in the Lab Setup Guide.

Activity

For this self-directed lab, determine the appropriate level of auditing for your environ-ment and then apply the auditing to the print devices that should be secured. The core process is the same as that used in the preceding lab, with one or two minor differences that will be self-evident.

Lab 15.7 Windows 2000 Security Template Concepts

Lab Scenario

To further enhance your security implementation, you would like to apply more restrictive security settings in Windows 2000. Ideally you would like a methodology that would allow you to apply the same security to computers and users, and have the settings re-applied at regular intervals throughout the day.

Objectives

The goal of this lab is to examine the range of options available through the Windows 2000 Security Templates. After completing this lab, you will be able to:

> ➤ Select the correct Security Template based on your organizational needs.

➤ Understand the variety of settings available through the pre-configured Security Templates.

➤ Know how to configure an MMC console to support the Security Templates.

Materials Required

This lab will require the following:

➤ Access to *Windows 2000 Server Resource Kit, Supplement 1*

➤ Access to a Windows 2000 Server with Active Directory installed

Activity Prerequisites

Lab is to be set up as stated in the Lab Setup Guide.

ACTIVITY

As your first step, you will need to populate an MMC Console with the Security Templates.

1. Click **Start**, click **Run**, and then type **mmc** and click **OK**. You will see the default view of a new, empty MMC console, as shown in Figure 15-14.

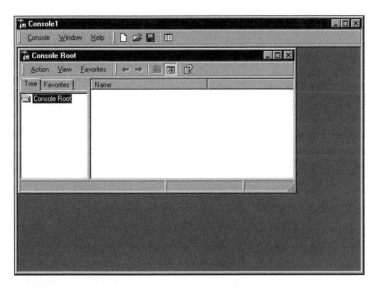

Figure 15-14   The default empty MMC console

2. Click the **Console** menu item and click **Add/Remove Snap-in**. See Figure 15-15.

3. Next click **Add**, scroll down the resulting list, and choose **Security Config-uration and Analysis** and **Security Templates**. (See Figure 15-16.) Select each snap-in one at a time by clicking the **Add** button and, when finished, click **Close**.

15

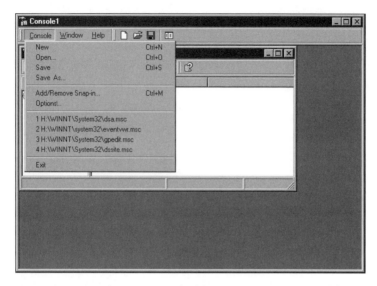

Figure 15-15   The process of adding a snap-in using Add/Remove Snap-in

Figure 15-16   The selection of the Security Configuration and Analysis snap-in

   4. Click **OK** once to return to the MMC Console. Maximize the MMC
      Console for best viewing. You should see a view similar to the one in
      Figure 15-17.

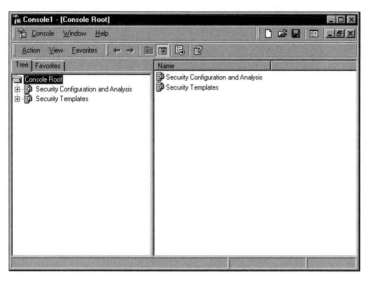

Figure 15-17   The new Security Configuration Analysis MMC tool

5. Now that the MMC is configured, click the **Console** menu and click **Save As**. Save as **Security** in the default path. When ready, click **Save**.

6. How many different Security Templates are there in this view?

7. As your next step in the lab, explore the different settings available to you for configuration. This step is in preparation for the next lab. When you are finished with this lab, leave the tool open since you will be using it in the next lab.

LAB 15.8 USING THE SECURITY CONFIGURATION AND ANALYSIS TOOL

Lab Scenario

The scenario for this lab is simple. You will use the MMC tool to configure security for a Windows 2000 environment.

Objectives

The goal of this lab is to learn how to use the Security and Configuration Tool for Security Template application. After completing this lab, you will be able to:

➤ Use the Security Configuration and Analysis Tool for securing Windows 2000 computers.

➤ Understand how to scan a computer for security variance.

➤ Know how to apply the corrective templates in a proactive, managed fashion.

15

Materials Required

This lab will require the following:

➤ Access to *Windows 2000 Server Resource Kit, Supplement 1*

➤ Access to a Windows 2000 Server with Active Directory installed

Activity Prerequisites

Lab is to be set up as stated in the Lab Setup Guide.

ACTIVITY

With the Security Configuration and Analysis Tool still open on your desktop, complete the following steps.

1. If the Security Templates tree is still expanded in the Console view, close it. You should now see the view shown in Figure 15-18.

2. Double-click the **Security Configuration and Analysis** tool to open the user interface and then follow the instructions to create a new database. Click **Open** to save the file when ready.

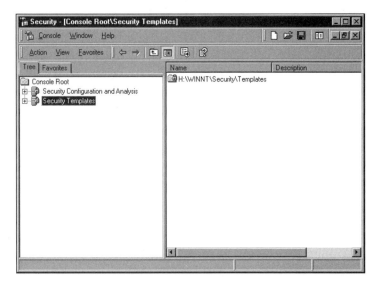

Figure 15-18   The default location of the Microsoft pre-configured Security templates

3. From the Import Template dialog box, choose the Security Template that you wish to test your computer against. In this example, the **securedc.inf** for a secure Domain Controller was selected. Once you have chosen a template, click **Open**. You will be returned to the main user interface. See Figure 15-19.

4. Now right-click **Security Configuration and Analysis.**You are now ready to analyze your computer. Click the **Analyze Computer Now** command and allow the process to continue. See Figure 15-20.

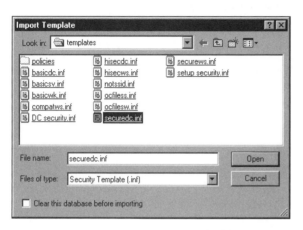

Figure 15-19 Selecting a pre-configured template

Figure 15-20 Beginning the process of analyzing security on the computer

5. You will see a screen similar to Figure 15-21 when the analysis process is running on your computer.

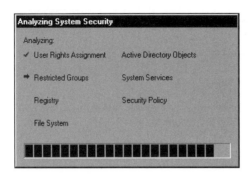

Figure 15-21   The Security Analysis progress bar

     6. When the process is complete, you may see a screen indicating where your security policy is in variance with Microsoft's predefined templates. Double-click an item to expand the view and see how to reconfigure your security settings to match the template. See Figures 15-22 and 15-23.

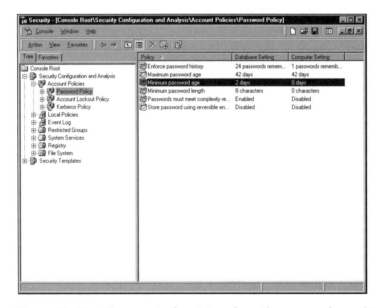

Figure 15-22   The report of variation from the pre-configured templates

Figure 15-23   Selecting one of the pre-configured options from the template

7. When you have finished your configuration adjustment, right-click **Security Configuration and Analysis** and choose the **Configure Computer Now** option. This will apply the new settings to your computer.

8. Leave the tool open since you will be using it for the next lab. This lab is now finished.

LAB 15.9 APPLYING PRE-CONFIGURED SECURITY TEMPLATES LOCALLY AND USING GPOS

Scenario

Now that you know how to configure the security templates using the Security Configuration and Analysis snap-in for Windows 2000, you will use the tool to design an implementation for your AD forest.

Objectives

The goal of this lab is to design an implementation of the Windows 2000 Security Templates for Windows 2000. You will use both the pre-configured templates, as well as templates that you have modified. You will need to take into consideration the following issues:

➤ Windows NT 4.0 Domain Controllers that have been upgraded to Windows 2000 Domain Controllers do not have any security configuration in place.

➤ You may need to apply more stringent security on your domain controllers.

➤ A decision has been made to apply the security templates to Windows 2000 Professional computers, not just Windows 2000 servers and domain controllers.

15

➤ Machines that belong to your domain should have the security settings reapplied several times during the day, at least every two hours.

➤ Domain controllers require that the security settings be reapplied at least twice every hour.

➤ Windows 2000 computers that do not belong to the domain also need the security templates applied in some way. They require the same refresh frequency as domain members.

After completing this lab, you will be able to:

➤ Apply the Windows 2000 security templates to domain clients through GPOs.

➤ Apply the Windows 2000 security templates to non-domain clients through individual applications.

➤ Modify the security templates to reflect changes specific to your environment.

➤ Plan the application of the security templates.

Materials Required

This lab will require the following:

➤ Access to *Windows 2000 Server Resource Kit, Supplement 1*

➤ Access to a Windows 2000 Server with Active Directory installed

Activity Prerequisites

Lab is to be set up as stated in the Lab Setup Guide.

ACTIVITY

This is a planning lab. Using the constraints listed in the Objectives section, design your implementation of the Windows 2000 Security Templates, taking into account all of the listed requirements above. This is a discovery lab. Be sure to utilize the *Windows 2000 Server Resource Kit, Supplement 1*. Create and apply your GPOs at the appropriate levels in AD and remember to design a solution for the computers, both Windows 2000 Professional and Windows 2000 Server, that do not belong to your domain. Be sure to assign specific roles to your design team members. Be prepared to explain your choices when you present to the class.